ITN's Best of Britain

edited by Lei Chatfield

Roger Ritchie, New York, NY

Martin Publications, Inc.
International Travel News

Martin Publications, Inc.
International Travel News
2120 28th Street • Sacramento, CA 95818
e-mail: itn@ns.net • www.intltravelnews.com

ISBN# 0-9675633-1-3

Foreword

It's our great pleasure to present this book about the British experience.

Different from other travel books you may encounter, the articles here were not written for a paycheck by "professional" travel writers.

Rather, these articles are straight from the heart — written for the sheer joy of sharing with other subscribers to ***International Travel News*** what the authors learned from their travels.

This book may prove to be a guide to those who still haven't availed themselves of a visit to Britain — one of the truly great destinations the planet has to offer.

Some may use this collection to relive memories. Others may find it useful in planning for a return visit.

On your next trip to Britain, should you find that some of the information we have presented is no longer correct — that a particular restaurant is gone or a hotel has changed hands — please drop us a note so that we may update further editions.

We can truly appreciate our readers' efforts expressed through the writing and photography presented here. The compilation of the articles into this book was a labor of love for its editor Lei Chatfield.

Cheers,

Armond M. Noble
Publisher, ***ITN***

Table of contents

London and about

England

England (con't)

Touring Britain

Discovering the charms of England, Scotland and Wales by auto, rail and boat.

Scotland

Wales

London and about

One of our day trips from London was to maritime Greenwich. The Royal Navy College was built in two halves, allowing an unobstructed view of the Thames from the Queen's House.

Cut-rate courier fares

Fortnight in London — some budget stretchers

PAT MITCHELL, Aptos, CA

How to spend less while traveling in order to afford more travel, that is the problem — deciding whether it is preferable to nurse a modest income at home or to satisfy a wanderlust by saving money while spending it.

A solution?

A courier flight perhaps? I decided to give it a try and joined the International Association of Air Travel Couriers (IAATC), scheduling a Jupiter flight to London. Itinerary, instructions and identifying logo arrived promptly after I paid the deposit and minimal airfare.

An overanxious first-timer, I arrived at the airport with my noncourier husband, Paul, well in advance of the specified time to meet a Jupiter representative. The logo was soon spotted and I was through check-in without delay. Everything went smoothly.

We had purchased London Visitor Travelcards before leaving and arranged a 2-week rental in **London Suites** apartments at Ovington Square. The rent, calculated out to $86 each per night, including maid service, was mitigated by preparing many of our own meals.

Food stores and the budget/diet-destroying Food Halls at Harrods were near and an in-house washer/dryer saved laundry costs and time.

The apartment is about four blocks from two Undergrounds: Piccadilly at Knightsbridge and the District and Central lines at South Kensington. It is also convenient to Brompton Oratory and the Victoria and Albert, a museum we especially enjoy.

The arrival

At Heathrow, following detailed courier instructions, I reported to an office about a block away.

After validating Travelcards we boarded the Piccadilly Underground, exiting via the multi-staired Harrods exit at Knightsbridge, then took a cab to Ovington Square.

We unpacked and then shopped, reacquainting ourselves with the neighborhood and its pub.

We have found that pubs offer good food at a reasonable price in a relaxed atmosphere with opportunities to meet local people. By the time we retired, we felt at home in London.

Walking about London

Next day we were ready for a "London Walk." Our introduction to the London of Shakespeare and Dickens was an informative 2-hour workout. Stimulated mentally and physically, we decided to take two more "walks," but not the same day.

We puzzled on our own through a web of byways in Southwark looking for Shakespeare's Globe Theatre.

Along the way we found beautiful Gothic/Norman Southwark Cathedral, photogenic ruins of Winchester Palace, and The Clink, now a museum but originally that place of incarceration whose name is now a generic term.

We finally located the recreated Globe in Bankside, entering past a poster picturing Shakespeare in a hard hat. Still under construction at the time of our visit, the theater is part of a complex intended as a study resource and workshop for actors.

Plans for a small indoor theater, designed by 17th-century architect Inigo Jones, have been disinterred and will be built as part of the complex.

The saving grace

On another day we used Travelcards to venture beyond Richmond to Ham House, an annex of the Victoria and Albert noted for its 17th-century furnishings.

The excursion challenged our flexibility with malfunctioning Underground signals, an aborted walk along a towpath made treacherous by slick high-tide deposits, and a No. 371 bus to the Ham House neighborhood that flashed past us.

We consoled ourselves in the *Fox and Duck* pub near the bus stop where we could happily have spent the afternoon, and should have. Ham House was closed, but the Fox and Duck remains a favorite memory.

Train tripping

After several days in museums, it was time for a day trip by train that allowed plenty of unfettered time to explore. I had compared standard-class train fares for four day trips from London and found that the Flexipass could save about $64.

For me, trains are almost a destination. They offer a rolling green panorama as well as being fast, comfortable and relatively safe, plus they generally drop passengers close to points of interest.

Our visit was in late October. Clouds, like those captured in Constable's paintings, piled themselves above the hills each morning. Evening rides featured spellbinding sunsets melting into an orange glow behind jagged purple silhouettes.

Bath day trip

My first day trip was to Bath. Trains leave Paddington Station every hour after 7:15 a.m. for a 1½-hour ride.

Paul chose to save Bath for a more in-depth visit, so I went to Paddington and exchanged my coupon for a Flexipass. For subsequent trips I needed only to fill in the date on the pass and board the train.

Bath is a stroller's paradise and it was an easy walk to the Roman baths. Five pounds bought an engrossing 2½-hour tour of gently bubbling pools, each in another shade of green, laid out among remnants of Roman architecture and sculpture.

From there a walk along colonnaded Bath Street was like stepping into the frontispiece of a time-worn book. The decayed charm of the Cross Bath attracted me. This tranquil spot, where Celts and Romans sought cures for ailments of the flesh, is being restored as a sanctuary.

Cambridge and York

We both took the next train trip to Cambridge. A Guide Friday bus delivered us close to Queens' College where I hoped to photograph an early 18th-century sundial.

The college was bolted shut and gray clouds seemed to blacken as we trudged on to King's College Chapel. Once there, high-spirited fan vaulting and brilliant stained-glass windows were the uplift we needed.

Later, under a bright sky, we passed Queens' College again. The gate was open though posted as "Closed." We went in and took the picture.

A train to York takes almost two hours from Kings Cross, too much for Paul, so he demurred in favor of memorizing the British Museum.

On arrival, a sunlit section of wall surrounding medieval York was inviting, but I resisted in favor of a fast, informative Guide Friday ride to York Minster.

Chilly air accelerated my entrance into a church made luminous by story-telling stained-glass windows. A doom stone in the crypt showing devils torturing the damned seemed the work of a Norman Michelangelo.

Roman, Saxon and Gothic artifacts compressed time amid underpinnings installed 25 years ago to save the church from collapse.

After two hours in York Minster, I meandered across town through narrow medieval streets in the eerie expectation I might meet the likes of Simple Simon or, preferably, the pieman. It was the savory wares of a pastry shop I sampled before moving on.

Again the past merged with the present. Perched on a knoll, the chilling ruin of Clifford Tower testified to fear-filled lives of early residents.

Maritime Greenwich

Careful planning for a fourth

day trip was for naught. There was no time to go to Oxford. The last Flexipass day was wasted on a one-way trip to Greenwich.

However, Greenwich was *not* a waste. We got off at Maze Hill and climbed to the observatory, straddled hemispheres, toured the Old Royal Observatory and Flamsteed House where we viewed Pluto (Disney's) through an antique telescope, then went downhill toward the dock, the *Cutty Sark* and the National Maritime Museum.

London Visitor Travelcards cover unlimited travel on public buses and subways as well as the Docklands Light Railway which runs from London's Bank or Tower Gateway stations to Greenwich.

In a special "All Hands" section for youngsters, aspiring stevedores honed their skills and signalpersons practiced semaphore while the young at heart snapped photos.

Home free

Suddenly, two weeks in London were reduced to memories. Since there was no courier package to carry back, I was not delayed in San Francisco.

Jupiter's Shirley Castro, who handled my trip arrangements, was patient and efficient, which helped to alleviate this initiate's jitters. My deposit check was returned promptly.

For *my* money, another "sale priced" courier flight is a great way to go. Free flights — generally last minute — are tempting, but my husband is not ready to answer the phone to hear, "Hi, honey. I'm in Singapore!"

Some essentials

Membership in the International Association of Air Travel Couriers includes a bimonthly bulletin listing available courier flights, fax updates and *The Shoestring Traveler*, a newsletter full of useful information on cheap stays and hints on getting around.

(IAATC's address is International Features, P.O. Box 1349 or 8 S. "J" St., Lake Worth, FL 33460-3742; phone 561/582-8320.)

Couriers are expected to dress neatly — no jeans and T-shirts. While my courier trip to London did not limit me to carryon luggage, a great many flights have such restrictions. (Believe one whose lessons have been hard; the art of packing light can be learned.)

Also, there is only one courier per flight, but couples can arrange courier flights on successive days. Length of stay varies and will be shown in listings.

•

London Visitor Travelcards cost $49 (1996) for seven consecutive days and must be purchased in the U.S. They cover unlimited travel on public buses and subway including Underground transfer from Heathrow on the Piccadilly line as well as Docklands Light Railway.

Flexipasses must be purchased in the U.S. Four days of standard-class Flexipass travel cost $175. For the trips I planned, the total regular fare would have been $239. I saved $36 and a minimal one-way fare to Greenwich.

We purchased Travelcards and Flexipasses at the California State Automobile Association.

•

The quiet London Suites apartment we have rented twice is accessible by stairs and cozy lift. The address is 12 Ovington Square, Knightsbridge, London SW3 1LN England; phone (44) (71) 581 5466 or fax (44) (71) 584 2912.

•

"The Original London Walks" and "Historical Walks of London" cost £4 (£3 for students and seniors). Brochures are readily available showing subject and meeting places.

•

Guide Friday city bus tours are available in many cities. Tickets are valid for the day and permit users to get on and off the bus at any stop. On-board tour guides lecture and answer questions.

Prices may vary slightly from city to city. Guide Friday in Cambridge charged £6.50 for adults, £4.50 for seniors and students and £2 for children five to 12. Look for discount coupons to enter some attractions as well as discount coupons for Guide Friday in other cities.

•

In Greenwich at *Trafalgar Tavern,* about two blocks from Queens House, we enjoyed an excellent dinner for £27.15 ($42.42 at £.64 = $1).

The return from Greenwich by boat to Westminster cost £4.80. Price varies by destination.

•

We had an outstanding Italian dinner at *Il Castelletto*, near the British Museum, for £32.35 ($50.55). The address is 17 Bury Place, London WC1A 21B; phone 0171-405 2232.

One free attraction in London is the changing-of-the-guard ceremony at Buckingham Palace. However, the "real" pomp and ceremony takes place across the way in front of the Wellington Barracks and Guards Museum. As the band and guard march out on their way to the palace, it is the opportune time for viewers to dash across St. James's Park to see the colorful horse guards approaching the palace from the other direction.

A wealth of sights at budget price — some of London's 'best bets'

LEI CHATFIELD, Senior Editor, ITN

A bargain late-January airfare — about $500 round trip from Sacramento to London — lured us to one of the most expensive cities on Earth. Cutting lodging costs by staying in an apartment rather than a hotel, we were determined to show that this city, my favorite, can be enjoyed at budget prices.

Serendipity

In pursuit of this delightful task, we met with serendipity: an indefatigable retiree, Mr. Husher, who led us on a merry chase showing us his city and proving that some of the best things in life — or at least London — are free or pretty inexpensive. . . even if a bit exhausting.

We met at the *real* changing-of-the-guard ceremony across the way from Buckingham Palace on Birdcage Walk at the Wellington Barracks and Guards Museum.

While my husband, John, was photographing the pomp and ceremony, which we didn't entirely understand, Mr. Husher approached and told us step-by-step what was happening, which regiment was participating in the ritual that day, etc.

After the band and guard marched out, he indicated that the short ceremony that was to follow at the palace was "for tourists."

Next, we were racing across St. James's Park to see the horse guards coming up the street from the other direction. At the last moment a horde of Japanese tourists was unleashed by their tour director to see this sight. Mr. Husher immediately diverted us across the street to see it unobstructed.

At this point I confessed I was writing a story about affordable London. After a few skeptical glances, we were led on our chase.

"Do you have a transport card?" he asked. We indeed had (our Travelcards were our first purchase at Heathrow Airport, but more on that later).

We soon were to learn all about the bus system (we already were proficient in the easy-to-learn Underground, or Tube, system). Though it's harder to figure out, the bus system is more relaxing and you get to see some of the city as you go.

Here's a bit of what Mr. Husher showed us that day: some of the best of London. Get some good guidebooks plus literature from the British Tourist Authority and take the time to see London. A lot can be seen on paid tours, but you can do it on your own for no more than the cost of a London Travelcard.

The chase

After whizzing by the Spencer home — "It's open for tours, now" — and learning about the security surrounding the royal residences, we were on a bus headed for the Strand and the City of London, the historic square mile and heart of old London.

There, we literally were run through the following (appropriately, I suppose, beginning on Fleet Street).

• The Royal Courts of Justice was our first stop; it's located just as you enter Fleet Street, which is the home to lawyers and journalists. The law courts look more like a cathedral than a public building.

Even if you don't have time to pop into one of the courts in session (quite interesting with the white-wigged barristers questioning witnesses standing in elevated witness stands) , do take the time to see the display of the costume and regalia of court.

It's located up the first flight of steps to the right after you pass security at the entrance — no cameras are allowed.

• Twinings of London tea shop — the original one — is just across the street if you want to pick up some gifts.

• The "Temple" is actually that area between Fleet Street and the Thames where barristers are trained and take up residence. The highlight there is a visit to Temple Church, dating from 1160, one of the earliest Gothic churches in England. Although damaged in WWII, there still are statues to 12th- and 13th-century knights on the floor of the church.

Working our way back up to Fleet Street, we peeked in at El Vino's pub, a staunch holdout for male-only patronage. One woman sued to be allowed to be served; she won but they refused her service at the bar; she sued again, said Husher, won again, and was served a drink at the bar. She left and never returned. The day we looked in, there wasn't a woman in sight.

• Ye Olde Cheshire Cheese on Wine Office Court has been in

business since 1538, rebuilt in 1667 after the Great Fire. There were plenty of professionals — both men and women — taking a break in this multilevel old pub. Take your pick for atmosphere: sawdust on the floor and ale, or a wine bar.

• St. Bride's Church is most interesting to visit for the layers of history visible there. Destroyed by the Great Fire and rebuilt by Christopher Wren, it later was destroyed in WWII (except for the tiered steeple after which wedding cakes today are patterned).

The crypt has an exhibit of the history of the church, including a Roman mosaic that predated the church. On the day we visited, a chamber ensemble was playing; free concerts regularly are held there.

• All we saw of St. Paul's was the outside corner as we waited under our umbrellas to catch the bus to the part of London Mr. Husher called home.

Shakespeare's & Dickens' London

We ended up at the Bankside district, home of Shakespeare's Globe Theatre, but our first stop was at London's oldest coaching inn, *The George* (Shakespeare's plays still are performed in its courtyard).

The George, London's oldest coaching inn, still has Shakespeare's plays performed in the courtyard.

It was there we finally spent our first pounds of the day, refreshing ourselves with some ale and a delightful nonalcoholic lime concoction.

Economical light meals are available there, too.

But time was wasting; we had yet to see St. Saviour's Church, where Shakespeare's brother is buried and where the founder of Harvard University was baptized. A schedule of free concerts is posted outside.

Winding down

As evening drew nigh, we took our last bus trip to the fashionable Chelsea district where we were shown the Chelsea Royal Hospital, founded in 1682 by King Charles II for veteran soldiers.

The building, another of Christopher Wren's, boasts an elegant banqueting hall. The chapel is open to the public and for Sunday services.

It was a cold afternoon, but in the summer visitors will see the veteran soldiers decked out in their scarlet coats and sitting in the vast courtyard. The hospital is open Monday to Saturday from 10 a.m. to noon and 2 p.m. to 4 p.m. and on Sunday, 2 p.m. to 4 p.m. Admission is free.

There's never a lack of things to do on a rainy day in London, including visiting the Tower of London to see the armor collection.

As we left the hospital, Mr. Husher pointed down the street, telling us that was where we'd find the National Army Museum, also free (ironic, as that is where we had planned to go that day — but we wouldn't have traded our revised day for anything).

London walks

We later found that many of the sights we had seen are included in walking tours of London. We took two of these tours; if you are not lucky enough to meet with your own Mr. Husher, I'd suggest taking advantage of these walks. Our tours were with The Original London Walks (P.O. Box 1708, London NW6 4LW; phone 0171-624-3978). They lasted about two hours and the experienced guides were excellent.

Our "Ghosts of the West End" guide, Graham, created the tour. Had he ever seen a ghost in 20 years? Only once: a disappearing lady in St. James's Park — thankfully, not the famous headless one purported to hang out there.

Not only did we wind through historic alleyways, but the minutiae that would be overlooked on a self-guided tour was pointed out by the guides: we started looking for the ghost of Samuel Pepys and in our imagination could see the torch bearers of years ago leading people safely home at night near Westminster.

After our "Old Westminster" afternoon walk, we attended the free and open-to-the-public evensong at Westminster Abbey, appreciating the choral concert by the red-robed choir boys. Evensong begins after the abbey is closed to tourist traffic for the day.

These walking tours, besides lending insight, are among the best bargains in town: £4 (a little over $6), or £3 for seniors. No reservations are required; just meet outside the designated Tube station at the designated time.

Some of the themes of the walks are Shakespeare & Dickens, Legal London, Covent Garden Pub Walk and the popular Jack the Ripper Haunts.

We found fliers for the London walks and dozens of other attractions in a rack as we entered our well-located apartment building (booked through Holiday Flatlets, 38 Emperor's Gate, London SW7 4HJ; phone 0171-589-2923, or fax 0171-373-6183).

The museums

Whatever your interest, London certainly has a museum to cater to it. Most have an entrance fee, but London's three premier art museums — the Tate Gallery, the National Gallery and the National Portrait Gallery — are free.

Then there's my favorite: the British Museum, tracing man's artistic and written history from Egypt's Rosetta Stone to Beatles' lyrics. Our friend, seeing the archaeological treasures — and especially the Rosetta Stone — for the first time, said, "This alone makes a trip here worthwhile." And, again, there's no admission charge.

Some of the liveliest free entertainment in London can be had at Speakers' Corner in Hyde Park near the Marble Arch. Anyone is welcome to bring a soapbox and preach on any subject that moves him. The fun starts at around 10 a.m. on Sundays.

Don't overlook Speakers' Corner

On Sundays, London s-l-o-w-s down. Don't plan on attending the theater, and that interesting restaurant you saw may well be closed, also. If you can't face another museum (they *are* open on Sundays), there's nothing more lively and fun to do than go to the "free theater" in Hyde Park near the Marble Arch.

Speakers' Corner is outrageous and at the same time very civilized. Since the late 1800s, those persons with a cause to promote have been able to bring out their soapboxes and preach on everything from politics to the virtues of vegetarianism.

On our visit there was a lively and entertaining man going on about the evil of the Torries; it was even more interesting when a conservative went head-to-head with him, with the crowd telling the conservative to get his own soapbox.

The show starts at about 10 a.m. and lasts until early afternoon.

Eating

Forget the horror stories of food in London. Like everything else, it's a matter of shopping around.

Try pub grub. Some is not so good, but we found a pub near our apartment that had great fish and chips — and the peas were not overcooked!

Also, ethnic restaurants offer some good meals (just avoid the "restaurant row" across from major hotels and you'll get some good meals at prices close to those you'd pay at home). Most restaurants post their menus outside.

The major supermarkets have some very good delis; neighborhood take-away shops also offer an inexpensive and tasty alternative.

Avoid the major hotel breakfasts unless you want to pay the equivalent of $14. There are plenty of small places around Victoria Station that have full English breakfasts for a fraction of the cost.

Getting around

For getting around London and environs I feel there's no better bet than the Travelcard.

The one that covers most of the sights that visitors to London would have time to see would be the Zones 1 and 2 card. This is good for Tube, bus and train travel in the majority of places in London.

Travelcards are available at Heathrow and major Tube stations; a passport photo is required,

The original Twinings Tea shop.

Hawker Hurricane at the RAF Museum in the suburb of Hendon.

but there are photo machines at the stations.

If you care to venture farther, you just show your card and pay a small supplement.

The card also is good for the Docklands Light Railway to Greenwich (from Tower Gateway to Island Gardens, then via Greenwich Foot Tunnel). If the city is closing in on you, this is a taste of small town (even though touristy). Stop by the tourist office to get information on walking tours.

We also took advantage of our Travelcard to venture out to Hendon (a supplement of £1 took care of the extra mileage) to see the RAF and Battle of Britain Museum. Signs at the exit direct you to the museum — within walking distance.

It has an incredible collection of planes — both Allied and German — but I most appreciated the tour in the Battle of Britain Museum led by a woman docent who was a child at the time London was being bombed.

There's a cafeteria serving light snacks and full lunches.

Summing up

I haven't touched on Covent Garden and the musicians you'll hear playing there. Nor have I mentioned the concerts at St. Martin-in-the-Fields Church near Trafalgar, the famous flea markets, Harrods sales. . . well, the list is endless. I guess someone said it before me: something along the lines of ". . . to be tired of London is to be tired of life."

I'm ready for the next discount airfare.

The Original London Walks

GERALD H. DESSNER, New York, NY

I spent a week in London in April '97. On my last day there, Monday the 28th, I decided to take a walking tour of Mayfair; it met at the Green Park Tube station at 10:30 a.m.

The cost, payable in cash to the guide on arrival, was £4.50 (US$7.45, at £1=US$1.65), or £3.50 ($5.80) for students, seniors and those who had taken other walks with The Original London Walks (phone 0171/624-3978).

Our guide, Graham, was listed as a boulevardier and bon vivant and the doyen of London's walking tour guides.

In a fast two hours he regaled us with tales of the aristocracy and their doings, pointing out a variety of famous mansions, mews and squares (such as Berkeley and Grosvenor), the American Embassy and **Claridge's Hotel** as well as a statue of Franklin Delano Roosevelt, who was beloved by the British in his day.

There are some 50 different walks available, listed by day and evening, offered in their brochure. This was a most pleasant way to see disparate parts of London and learn more about its history.

Select few witness key ceremony at Tower of London

JUDY NIEMAM, San Angelo, NM

While the Tower of London is a popular tourist attraction, most of its approximately 2.3 million annual visitors never see it at night — certainly not from the inside.

But each night of the year, except Dec. 24-26 and New Year's Eve, some 70 persons are granted entrance to the Tower precincts to witness one of the oldest military ceremonies in the world — the 700-year-old Ceremony of the Keys — during which the main gates of this most-famous royal palace and fortress are locked.

In their footsteps. .

At 9:35 p.m., a scarlet-coated yeoman warder, one of the retired British military men appointed to special duty at the Tower, guides ticket-holders through the outer gates and down the cobblestone road to an area between the inner wall and Traitors' Gate.

When the River Thames was used to transport prisoners between Westminster, where they were tried, and the Tower, where they were imprisoned or executed, Traitors' Gate was the landing place and entrance.

Think of the historic figures – Sir Thomas More, Thomas Cromwell and Queen Anne Boleyn, among them – who passed through this gate on their way to a fateful end. Perhaps you're standing in their very footsteps. It's been said that some in ghostly form still roam the grounds.

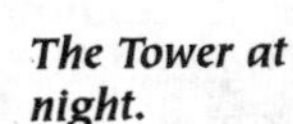

The Tower at night.

Locked in

"This is not a tourist attraction," the yeoman warder assured those of us fortunate enough to attend the little-known, late-night ritual (this fact impressed our 11-year-old grandson who attended with my husband and me).

The ceremonial locking-up didn't even stop for World War II, although for their safety the guardsmen were permitted to wear steel helmets in place of their usual headgear.

It has considerably more pomp than our own nightly locking-up in our homes, but it is, nevertheless, nothing more than that.

Although it's the chief yeoman warder, or his deputy, who locks the gates, he is accompanied by an escort from the Tower Guard, the military regiment that protects Buckingham Palace and St. James Palace as well as the Tower of London.

En route to Queen's House to return the keys for safekeeping, he's challenged by an armed sentry. After a loud, rapid-fire exchange of questions and answers, the locking-up detail – and the keys – are given permission to pass through the inner wall with the onlookers following.

In case you haven't realized that you have been locked inside the Tower, your guide will, undoubtedly remind you.

"But you needn't worry," he adds. "There is enough accommodation for all."

The drummer

At the bottom of the steps that lead up to Waterloo Barracks and the White Tower, the detail halts. Another contingent of guardsmen stands on the steps while a lone musician at the top plays "The Last Post."

"Did you hear the drummer?" asks the escort.

"What drummer?" we wondered. "That's a bugler!"

Noticing the bewildered glances among the visitors, the escort explains that "The Last Post" was played by a drummer until about 200 years ago, when a bugler took over the job.

"But," he smiles, "we English are slow to accept change, so we still call him the drummer."

As for being locked inside the Tower. . . however much you might welcome the unexpected adventure of remaining overnight, you will be escorted back to the locked outer gate.

There, you'll depart by stepping through a small door, called a wicket, set in each of the main gates.

As you bid good night to your escort, don't forget to whisper farewell to Queen Anne Boleyn and the fortress' other ghostly residents who might have walked silently in your midst during this very special visit to the Tower of London.

Arranging a visit

There's no charge to observe the ceremony, but tickets are required. Apply several weeks before your trip by writing to the Ceremony of the Keys Clerk, Waterloo Block, HM Tower of London, London EC3N 4AB, England, listing several alternate dates.

To cover the cost of return postage, include an International Response Coupon, available from the post office.

Photography, videotaping and recording are strictly prohibited before, during and after the ceremony.

The haunts of Rumpole — exploring 'legal London'

DENNIS A. CAVAGNARO, Oakland, CA

"Rumpole of the Bailey" has been welcomed into our homes at least six times a year for the past 10 years or so via television.

Rumpole, this rumpled, put-upon but ultimately vindicated and victorious barrister (roughly equivalent to a trial lawyer in the U.S.) has made such an impact that the character long ago inspired the formation of a devotee club, The Rumpole Society.

As visitors to London, we can spend a day or more exploring easily on foot the real, fictional and semifictional sites haunted by Rumpole or his creator, John Mortimer.

A bit about Rumpole

While Rumpole is fictional, the Old Bailey and many of his haunts on Fleet Street and in legal London are there for us to discover and to enrich our appreciation for the freedoms we enjoy and, sadly, often take for granted.

Though Rumpole practices law in England, he probably teaches us more about the law and its philosophy than any of our highly publicized trials.

Perhaps Rumpole's popularity owes to the low esteem in which we seem to hold the legal profession. We don't trust lawyers, but we fiercely believe in the fictional Rumpole.

We men secretly identify with Horace Rumpole as he struggles through life enduring the taunts of his wife, the formidable Hilda, "She Who Must Be Obeyed," a Q.C.'s (Queen's Counsel's) daughter who assumed Rumpole would also climb in the legal profession and "take the silk" as a Q.C.

A self-confessed "Old Bailey hack," Rumpole is continually belittled by his professional colleagues. In court he must battle not only smug and overconfident prosecutors enjoying the full support of the state but often the judges as well.

To the fellow members of his chambers (not a partnership but a shared law office) he's an embarrassment with his rumpled dress, his obvious disdain for irrelevant protocol and his practice — though successful — of defending petty criminals and the lower antisocial classes.

New York Times critic John J. O'Connor characterizes Rumpole wonderfully: "We are left then with Rumpole tilting at the world's windmills of stuffiness and hypocrisy. When necessary, he invokes immortal lines from Shakespeare or Wordsworth or Keats. Rising with boozy majesty to just about any occasion, he can disarm hostile forces with the sheer sweep of his arguments."

In search of Rumpole

Where better to look for Rumpole than in the Old Bailey itself? It is an appropriately dignified edifice of Portland stone, with a dome surmounted by a figure of Justice robed in gold. Inscribed over the principal doorway are the words "Defend the children of the poor and punish the wrongdoer."

Anytime you sit on a jury or are judged by a jury, you owe a huge debt to the Old Bailey. On the ground floor, next to the main entrance — which, unfortunately, due to security considerations, is now closed to the general public — is a marble tablet commemorating the 17th-century jury which established the inalienable right of jurors to give a verdict according to their own conclusions.

It reads, "Near this site William Penn and William Mead were tried for preaching to an unlawful assembly in Gracechurch Street.

"This tablet commemorates the courage and endurance of the Jury, Thos. Vere, Edward Bushell and ten others who refused to give a verdict against them, although locked up without food for two nights and fined for their verdict of Not Guilty."

Penn (yes, for whom Pennsylvania is named), Mead and the 12 jurymen had been committed to Newgate Prison until they had paid their fines — Penn and Mead for contempt of court and the jurymen for opposing the will of the court and standing their ground.

The case of the jurymen, however, was reviewed by a writ of habeas corpus, the plea being for wrongful imprisonment, and the judgment of the court was unanimous in favor of the prisoners and jurymen.

Visitors are allowed to observe the cases being heard and they queue up daily while the court is in session at the Newgate Street entrance. While Rumpole may not be physically present, his peers are there.

To make the experience more memorable, attend the morning session and then take lunch at one of the surrounding pubs: a new version of *Magpie and Stump*, the cleverly named *Rumbo's* on Old Bailey Road or the *Viaduct Tavern* on Newgate.

For one pound the publican will lead you on an underground tour of some evil-looking cells — dungeons — claimed to be from the infamous Newgate Prison which was pulled down to make way for the Old Bailey. You'll require a pint to exorcise the ghosts.

Old Bailey's starring roles

Courtroom drama in the Old Bailey can be as riveting as any played in the theaters, with one notable plus: it's real. It's also free.

To Rumpole's creator, the Old Bailey "offers more drama to the dedicated visitor than the West End and Broadway put together, but the theatrical pace is slow, the seats not always comfortable and the sightlines not always good. Executions cannot be watched from the Magpie and Stump anymore, but the spectacle of human suffering is always public."

My wife and I first visited the Old Bailey as tourists in August 1975. We looked forward only to seeing the red-robed judge and the barristers and members of the court in their black robes and powdered wigs.

Unfortunately, it was during a particularly ugly time, as London and the surrounding area were suffering random terrorist bombings. Security was heavy. We got more drama than we could have imagined.

We hoped to observe a case in Courtroom One. As soon as we were allowed through the Newgate Street entrance we were subjected to body searches. Unbeknownst to us, the case was the trial of the so-called Guildford Four.

The young men and women were on the docket. We made eye contact. To us, comfortably in the middle class, they just did not look like criminals. My wife said at the time, "They couldn't have done it."

Much to our surprise, her intuition was confirmed when 15 years later they were found to have been unjustly convicted and were released. When we watched the award-winning Daniel Day Lewis film "In the Name of the Father," we were shocked to realize "that was our case."

Of course, the Old Bailey "starred" in "In the Name of the Father" and in many other films as well, among them "Witness for the Prosecution" and "A Fish Called Wanda."

Legal haunts

If Rumpole had already slipped away from the Old Bailey, perhaps we could find him shopping for a wig and gown. He'd be in Ede and Ravenscroft, Ltd., "Legal Wig Makers since 1726."

If you can't find Rumpole about this hallowed emporium, you may at least safely guess that many of the other patrons are judges, barristers and other members of the courts. Take a peek into the store. At least one mannequin on the floor is done up in legal regalia.

It's as good a place as any in London to find men's furnishings.

This writer took home a quality umbrella with "Ede and Ravenscroft" engraved on the shaft.

Just around the corner we might

find Rumpole browsing through the stacks of London's foremost legal bookseller, Wildy & Sons, Ltd., established 1830. This cozy bookstore occupies both sides and straddles the archway leading into Lincoln's Inn.

The shop also carries whimsical legal cartoon art. I came away with a popular cartoon found on the walls of many an American attorney's office.

While at Wildy's, step through the archway into Lincoln's Inn. You'll notice bewigged and cloaked barristers hurrying to and fro. Blink your eyes and allow the peace and architecture of the place to magically transport you to Oxford or Cambridge.

The Public Records Office Museum in the same neighborhood on Chancery Lane is worth a browse. It holds the "Domesday Book," Shakespeare's will, Nelson's and Wellington's logs and dispatches.

Continue down Chancery Lane, cross Fleet Street and walk a few steps east to *El Vino's*. Surely, if Rumpole were relaxing between briefs, we'd find him here, the inspiration for his fictional *Pommeroy's*.

In Rumpole's own words, "What can I say in defense of this venerable institution, second only in my affections to my regular wine bar, Pommeroy's? It is still a bastion of the male establishment little affected by a decade of Women's Liberation. Females are tolerated only so long as they sit in a small area set aside for their use."

Alas, El Vino's doesn't carry a bottle of Rumpole's favorite, "Chateau Thames Embankment," but the atmosphere is "legal London." Gents, remember to wear a suit and tie. Observe the action at luncheon. The sandwiches — roast English topside of beef and watercress — are ample.

The Wig & Pen

Back up to the top end of Fleet Street and close by the Inner Temple Lane opening to Rumpole's chambers, the *Wig & Pen Club* is housed in a cozy, 17th-century building. While epitomizing our notion of an exclusive London club, it's now open to all.

While the legal profession ("Wig") remains in the neighborhood, the great newspapers ("Pen") have fled to the Docklands.

The Wig & Pen Club was the only Strand building to survive the Great Fire of London in 1666.

This quaint building was erected in 1625 and was the only Strand building to survive the Great Fire of London in 1666.

With its assortment of tiny dining rooms and meeting rooms, narrow stairways, nooks and crannies, the club is a treasure trove of newspaper, artistic and political memorabilia. Famous front pages from around the world, witty cartoons and caricatures, original prints and personal notes from the famous grace the walls.

Try a meal, as the club continues to honor typical English fare in season: shepherd's pie, tripe and onions, boiled beef and dumpling, Lancashire hot pot with red cabbage, spotted dick and custard and more, including that old staple, steak and kidney pie.

Rumpole's neighborhoods

A few steps away, duck through the portal of the timbered Dr. Johnson's Buildings. If you look through the window of No. 1 you might see Horace Rumpole's hat hanging on the wall. These are the chambers (aka Rumpole's chambers at No. 3 Equity Court) where John Mortimer was based when he began to write "Rumpole of the Bailey."

Perhaps we can catch Rumpole stopping into S. Weingott and Son, the famous Fleet Street cigar and wine emporium where, according to Rumpole, "I purchase a pack of budget cigars and a bottle of superior Bordeaux." The shop is much as Rumpole has described it but has changed hands and been renamed Four Vintners.

Though Rumpole hasn't described it (it's been open only a year), cross the Strand to look into one of the world's most beautiful pubs, the *Olde Bank of England*. The elegant "eating and drinking emporium" occupies the Bank of England's former Law Courts Branch, a 106-year-old building.

As many of the safe and vault doors as possible have been retained, including two walk-in safes in the kitchen. Additional ironwork was commissioned to match the front gates. The bar counter is solid granite. One can hope that Rumpole and Mortimer will discover this pub, a gold-plated beauty.

While it wouldn't be proper to follow Rumpole home to his flat, "Casa Rumpole," the lair of "She Who Must Be Obeyed," at 2a Froxbury Mansions, Gloucester Road, we can imagine it by accommodating ourselves in the same neighborhood at **The Gore Hotel**.

The Gore, a private hotel since 1908, was formerly the townhouse of a member of the Marquess of Queensbury's family. The small, elegant hotel is just a stone's throw from Kensington Gardens and the Royal Albert Hall and only a 5-minute ride from Harrods.

It's served by the Gloucester Road Tube station where, if our timing is right, we might just catch a glimpse of Horace Rumpole on his daily commute. Good hunting.

Rumpole's musings

While we take Rumpole seriously, his is a more jaundiced view: "Such notoriety will not long survive my not-to-be-delayed trip to Golders Green Crematorium. Barristers' speeches vanish quicker than Chinese dinners, and even the greatest victory in Court rarely survives longer than the next Sunday's papers."

Checklist

For information on visiting London and Great Britain, write British Tourist Authority, 551 Fifth Ave., Ste. 701, New York, NY 10176-0799; phone 800/462-2748

Address book

Here's a list of addresses to help you find the aforementioned establishments.

• *Viaduct Tavern*, 126 Newgate Street, London EC1; phone (0171) 606-8476.

• Ede & Ravenscroft, Ltd., 93 Chancery Lane, London WC2A 1DU; phone (0171) 405-3906.

• Wildy & Sons, Ltd., Lincoln's Inn Archway, Carey Street, London WC2A 2JD; phone (0171) 242- 5778.

• The Public Records Office Museum, Chancery Lane, London WC2A 1LR; phone (0181) 787-6344.

• *El Vino's*, 47 Fleet Street, London WC4; phone (0171) 353-6786.

• *Wig & Pen Club*, 229/230 Strand, London WC2R 1BA; phone (0171) 583-7255.

• *Four Vintners* (formerly S. Weingott and Son), 3 Fleet Street, London EC4Y 1AU; phone (0171) 583-2472.

• *The Olde Bank of England*, 194 Fleet Street, London EC4; phone (0171) 430-2255.

• **The Gore Hotel**, 189 Queen's Gate, London SW7 5EX; phone (0171) 584-6601.

(Note: from the United States, call London telephone numbers by dialing 011-44-171, then the seven digits. Drop the first 0 of the London area code (i.e., 0171 or 0181) when calling there internationally.)

---

or 212/986-2200.

For books, tapes, videos and whimsical souvenirs on Rumpole, write to the not-for-profit Rumpole Society. Quite regularly the society invites to dinner John Mortimer and members of the cast and creative staff. Alas, Leo McKern, who plays Rumpole, doesn't fly, but perhaps he will call one day on a *QE2* 'round-the-world cruise.

Write to the Rumpole Society, P.O. Box 906, San Mateo, CA 94403.

Annual membership is $25. Semiannual dinners are usually held in May and October in San Francisco.

Rumpoliana includes "The Rumpole Cook Book," "She Who Must be Obeyed" nightshirts and T-shirts, and "Chateau Thames Embankment" and "Pommeroy's Plonk" wine labels.

Visting the Old Bailey

For viewing trials at the Old Bailey (to be correct, the Central Criminal Court) when it is in session, queue at the Newgate Street entrance. A sign outside lists the day's hearings. The Public Gallery is open weekdays from 10:30 a.m. to 1 p.m. and from 2 p.m. to 4 p.m.; phone (0171) 248-3277.

John Mortimer offers a bit of advice: "The Public Galleries are one way to see Old Bailey trials, but the visitor would be better advised to get an introduction to a barrister or solicitor (the behind-the-scenes lawyer) to get a seat in the well of the court rather than the gallery. The acoustics are better and you may feel more intimately connected with the trial."

Legal London walking tour

Visitors might wish to join the regularly scheduled — in sunshine and/or rain — walking tour of "Legal London." The excellent tour guides will pass the Old Bailey and describe it as well as the Newgate Prison and the history of criminal and civil justice in London.

The tour also visits and explores the Royal Courts of Justice, Gray's Inn, Lincoln's Inn, the Temple and Middle Temple, passing John Mortimer's law chambers at 1, Dr. Johnson's Buildings.

Contact Original London Walks, P.O. Box 1708, London NW6 4LW, England; phone (0171) 624-3978.

I recommend that you detour a few blocks from the Old Bailey, across Newgate Street and up Gillespie Street alongside St. Bartholomew's Hospital to one of the oldest (1123) surviving churches in London, the medieval Norman St. Bartholomew-the-Great. Religious or not, you will be moved by its humble majesty and tranquility.

The opening of Parliament in London

LLOYD McCUNE, Contributing Editor

Anyone in London in November and wanting to see part of this spectacle when the Irish State coach passes should join other bystanders along the route between Buckingham Palace and the Houses of Parliament.

Taking place in November, the opening of Parliament is the ceremony when the Queen reads, from the throne in the House of Lords, the government's program for the coming year.

For this occasion the Queen travels from Buckingham Palace in a coach drawn by horses to the Victoria Tower in the Houses of Parliament. There she descends from the coach and enters the Robing Room, where she puts on the crimson robe and the Imperial State Crown.

She then proceeds to the House of Lords, where robed lords, judges, peeresses and members of the Diplomatic Corps await her.

Royal rebuff — It is with regret that I repeat a news item read in a London paper early in June, a notice I have not found in any other European paper: the Queen, who was scheduled to open a new educational building in Wales, had to forgo this appointment at the last minute due to students who were preparing a barrage of eggs.

Here I am reminded of a proverb found in a French provincial paper: "*Bon sens etieunesse ne vontjamais ensemble*" ("Good sense and youth never go together").

Houses of Parliament along the Thames.

England and London's treasures

CARTER CLEMENTS, Contributing Editor

It's always a joy for me to return to England, where most traveling Americans feel at home and in tune with many things, including, of course, the language! Adding to my enjoyment this time was the speedy new way of getting there from France, by way of the Chunnel.

Some thoughts about the Chunnel trip

If time is of the essence during your trip and you have to visit both England and the mainland of Europe, this is the way to go!

Leave the driving to someone else and forget about problems with fog, bad weather, airport congestion or questionable ferry sailings. You can kick back, relax, have a drink or something to eat, snooze, or just catch up on your notes about your itinerary.

In just a couple of hours, you've made the transition to another country and lifestyle in just about the most comfortable way possible as well as saved yourself some valuable hours you can put to better use.

Arranging for your reservations is pretty simple; you can do it all in the States before you begin your trip by getting in touch with your travel agent, BritRail (800/677-8585), Eurostar (800/EUROSTAR) or RailEurope (800/4-EURAIL).

The folks at any of these places will answer your questions, inform you of available options which might assist you in planning your trip, make your reservations and set it all up so you embark from America with reservations, tickets, train and seat assignments and a feeling of getting it all done in one fell swoop!

All train cars on Eurostar are air-conditioned and have spacious seats with reading lamps and foot rests. There is a buffet bar; lunch or dinner can be served right at your seat, and there are even train-to-shore public telephones available should you wish to call someone and let them in on what you are doing!

Britain highlights by rail

Now to some of this nation's "treasure spots for visitors" which also may be easily reached by train (BritRail).

WINDSOR CASTLE — just 21 miles from London.

A residence of the Queen, and started in its construction over 900 years ago by William the Conqueror, the castle alone has a community of over 350 people living and working within its walls.

It's a good place to get a fine look at the history of the British Empire, some great art and the ever-popular "changing of the guard."

Take the train to Windsor from Paddington Station, London.

CANTERBURY — about an hour away by rail, and called by many the center of Christianity since the year 597. The famous cathedral and the old city walls are of special interest, as are many fascinating old homes and shops in town.

Use the train from London's Victoria Station.

OXFORD — also about an hour away by rail.

This popular university city has lots of historical buildings and ivy-covered college structures. It's a fairly easy town to wander around in by foot, and there are plenty of neat little things to see and do.

ARUNDEL — slightly more than an hour south of London by train.

This great little town in Sussex, complete with a wonderful castle of its own, will give you a pretty good feeling for Olde England and life away from the big city. There are some interesting buildings, shops AND pubs.

BRIGHTON — 50-some miles south of London.

This famous beach resort is a popular place for those from the big city to spend their weekends out of town. There are lots of Victorian-style homes as well as shops plus things to see and do.

London bits

I would be hard-pressed to mention all of the great attractions in just one story; instead, let me name a few more and trust that they will whet your appetite for others as well.

TOWER OF LONDON — Situated right on the north bank of the Thames River and easily reached by subway (Tube) by getting off at the Tower Hill Station, this is one of the major attractions which has plenty of English history attached.

Begun by William the Conqueror, the compound actually has a number of towers, and in many of them the famous and infamous have been imprisoned and/or killed down through the centuries.

If you are into ghosts of times past or the famous "ravens," a museum of old weapons and instruments of torture or the crown jewels, don't miss this place.

The famous "Beefeaters" (guards) look after the compound, and tours of approximately one hour are conducted every 30 minutes or so. For about US$20 you can get the full treatment and it's well worth it!

WESTMINSTER ABBEY, which dates back to at least 1066, looks out over Parliament Square and is the spot where the leaders of the nation have always been crowned, with the two exceptions of Edward V and Edward VIII.

Many of England's "greats" are

entombed there as well, and the Early Gothic structure has a number of beautiful and interesting chapels, including one dedicated to the memory of the RAF heroes of World War II.

The museums and gardens adjoining the abbey are treasures in themselves and a visit is a must if you are really into British history. Take the subway to Westminster Station.

BUCKINGHAM PALACE and ST. JAMES PALACE may also be reached by getting off at the Westminster Tube stop and walking through some of the prettiest parts of London, including Green Park and St. James Park.

Also in this vicinity, and actually closer to the north bank of the Thames River, are the famous HOUSES OF PARLIAMENT and the tower containing BIG BEN, the clock which seems to epitomize the spirit of England and its long history.

As I said in the beginning, these are but a few of the more interesting spots in this great city and the British Tourist Authority offices in the United States and the local offices in London itself will be happy to provide you with all the necessary information to locate and visit those YOU may wish to see.

London city tour

One of the great ways to get a quick look at London and possibly decide which attractions you want to spend more time at is by utilizing a tour.

One I would highly recommend is called the "ORIGINAL LONDON TRANSPORT SIGHTSEEING TOUR," which is fairly inexpensive, as tours here go, and is usually made in one of those big, red, double-decker buses.

You may catch this tour at any one of four spots in central London, including Victoria Station, Piccadilly Circus, Marble Arch or the Baker Street Tube station.

There usually is no official guide on this tour, but a map of your route is provided and the driver will usually call out the salient points and provide some interesting information regarding each one.

London is a sprawling city where plenty of history, tradition and ceremony blend together with some awe-inspiring sights. The double-decker bus is a great way to get a good, early glimpse of a good part of it all.

The tour will take you past Hyde Park and Green Park, Buckingham Palace, St. James Palace and Westminster Abbey. It will cross the River Thames three or four times, and the views of the city and the opportunities for photos from these vantage points are excellent.

For example, Lambeth and Westminster bridges give you a good look at the Houses of Parliament and Big Ben, and from Waterloo Bridge you will glimpse the spires of many of the city's famous churches and the dome of St. Paul's Cathedral.

Later on the tour you will pass directly in front of St. Paul's, where Lord Nelson, the Duke of Wellington and Christopher Wren are entombed, to mention but a few.

From the roadway at Tower Bridge, you can see the imposing Tower of London itself, and later on you will see the Royal Exchange and Mansion House, the official residence of the Lord Mayor of London.

You also will pass by Downing Street (location of the home of the British Prime Minister), colorful Trafalgar Square and Piccadilly Circus, which is known as the hub of the west end of London and features outstanding theater and nightlife.

London Transport also operates more extensive tours of the city, ranging from full- and half-day excursions to evening and boat tours on the Thames. Many of these tours depart from Victoria Station, as do some out-of-town runs to places like Oxford, Bath, Stonehenge and Brighton.

For a quick look at most of the major sights of London before you decide what merits your closer scrutiny, I would recommend the "Original London Transport Sightseeing Tour."

Gallery of the House of Commons, London

LLOYD McCUNE, Contributing Editor

The Strangers' Gallery is open while the House is in session, usually in the afternoon from 2:30 p.m. to 10 p.m. on Mondays, Tuesdays, Wednesdays and Thursdays and from 9:30 a.m. till 3 p.m. on most Fridays.

To check on whether the House will be in session, phone 0171-219-4272, or listen to the recorded announcement of business by calling 0171-219-5532.

Visitors should apply to their Embassy for a card of introduction (Americans to the American Embassy, Canadians to their High Commissioner).

It should be noted that no more than four cards may be issued on any one day, so visitors may find cards only available for several weeks ahead.

Cards do not guarantee entry at 2:30 p.m. Often, card bearers will not be admitted until after Question Time, which is after 3:30 p.m.

If one does not have a card, one may join the public queue outside St. Stephen's Entrance, where a wait of one to two hours is common during the afternoon.

In any case, all visitors should go to the ST. STEPHEN'S ENTRANCE, the main entrance to the Houses of Parliament (also called "Palace of Westminster"), which is located in the center of the Palace of Westminster, opposite the east end of Westminster Abbey.

The nearest Underground station is Westminster, or take buses 3, 11, 12, 24, 53, 77A, 88, 109, 159, 184 or 511. Though a car park is available (Abingdon Street), it often is full; visitors would be well advised to use only public transportation.

Tours of the Palace of Westminster — for a separate leaflet giving details of how to obtain a tour of the Houses of Parliament, call the Public Information Office, House of Commons, at 0171-219-4272.

This number is worth noting if one desires any information concerning a visit to the House when some sessions sit until 10:30 p.m. or later.

Changing of the guard — Windsor Castle.

London outings — Windsor, boat trips & Hampton Court

GERALD H. DESSNER, New York, NY

Visiting Windsor Castle and Eton College

On a Wednesday in April '97, I took a day trip with friends in London to visit Windsor Castle and, later, Eton College across the river.

We took the 10:18 a.m. train from Paddington Station direct to Windsor; this cost £5.20 (US$8.50 at £1=US$1.63) round trip.

It was a pleasant ride, less than 40 minutes, and we arrived in time to watch the changing of the guard — less pomp than at Buckingham Palace but nonetheless quite thrilling.

We purchased a Windsor entrance ticket for £9.80 ($16) and proceeded to visit Queen Mary's Doll House, St. George's Chapel, the State Apartments and the

Albert Memorial Chapel. There still were signs from the fire a few years ago, and the castle is still being restored.

After a hot lunch and a Murphy Stout at a pub in town, we journeyed by foot across the river to Eton, a pleasant little town.

On the quaint streets that lead to the college, we ran into groups of Eton students dressed in their striped morning coats and tails but with no top hats.

We paid the £2.50 ($4) entrance fee to see some of Eton indoors, including the chapel, where a choir rehearsal was going on, and the Eton museum with information about famous graduates such as Shelley, Goldsmith and others, including Henry VI (the college was founded in 1440).

We wandered about for some time and left for the Windsor station in order to catch our 4:09 p.m. return train to Paddington by way of Slough. It was a pleasant experience and a glimpse into an earlier era.

Canal boat ride, London-Little Venice

A friend and I took the Bakerloo Underground line to the Warwick Avenue station in London early on Friday, April 25, '97, to purchase tickets for the 12:30 p.m. Jason's Trip canal boat ride to Little Venice (phone 0171-286-3428). The tickets cost £5.5, or US$9, per person, round trip.

We had an hour to spare and so we enjoyed a wonderful lunch and a glass of Chardonnay at *Jason's Restaurant* right there on the dock.

My friend ordered a bowl of *moules*, or mussels, that came heaped and steaming in a wonderful tomato-based sauce with some fresh, crunchy French bread to help soak it up.

I had a dish of cold chicken and salad. The salad had the best lettuce variety I can remember and a wonderful dressing. The chicken was quite tasty, too. That may have been the best meal we had during our week in London. It cost £20, or $33, for both of us.

The day was cloudy, cool and a bit wet, so there were only about 10 passengers on the long and narrow boat that seated 69. These boats originally were used to carry all sorts of cargo around London and originally were pulled by ropes attached to horses that trudged along the banks.

The crew consisted of two sailors, the captain and his mate plus a guide who told us about the canals, locks and sights along the way. She also offered drinks and food to the passengers.

We saw some lovely mansions set along the water's edge and some beautiful weeping willow trees as well as a few restaurants. After an hour we stopped at Camden, where some passengers disembarked and newcomers arrived.

You can take the Underground home from that stop instead of returning by boat as we did. There was no commentary on the way back and the rain became quite heavy along the route. We were protected by a canopy that was lowered, so we stayed fairly dry.

The round trip took less than two hours and was quite a pleasant experience, although you might as well get off at Camden and wander around the shops and then return by Underground.

Should you take this trip, arrive

early enough to enjoy the wonderful bill of fare at Jason's Restaurant.

Thames half-day cruise

A friend and I bought tickets at London's Westminster Pier (phone 0171-930-4097, Westminster Underground Station) on Sunday morning, April 27, '97, for a 10:30 a.m. riverboat ride on the Thames to Hampton Court.

It was a 3½-hour, slow and lazy ride up the Thames that stopped along the way at Kew and Richmond. The cost was £12, or $19.80, round trip (figuring £1=US$1.65).

On board they sold both soft drinks and hard drinks plus sandwiches, cakes, etc., at the bar, where we could sit indoors at tables. On the open deck on top we could see all the sights in the fresh air. It was a beautiful, sunny day; we even got a bit of a suntan.

Along the way we passed under many bridges, each with a story related by the on-board tour guide over the loudspeaker. We also saw gentle Sunday afternoon leisure life in many towns.

There were an unusual number of rowers in skulls and kayaks, some in teams with coaches following and exhorting them on in motorcraft. Some became annoyed at the wake that our boat produced and shook their fists at us. Usually, they just accepted the slight inconvenience.

On the way up, we went through two locks — a miniature Panama Canal experience — but on the way back we went through only one; we supposed this was because the river had risen enough to not need the lock services twice.

We arrived at Hampton Court a bit late, about 2:20 p.m. and had to rush to see some of the displays, as the last boat back to Westminster left at 4 p.m. It would have been possible to return by BritRail (and at a much faster pace), but we chose the river.

The entrance fee, with concessions (as they call it) for older people, was £6.40, or $10.55. In our limited time there, we visited the Clock Court, the King's Apartments, the Queen's Gallery, the fascinating Tudor Kitchens and the spectacular formal gardens.

The kitchens were most interesting because they were stocked with fowl, meat, spices, etc., of the 16th century, such that you could actually imagine dining there.

Back aboard the *Connaught*, we left the dock promptly at 4 p.m. The return trip was a bit faster; we arrived at Westminster Pier just before 7 p.m. It was a delightful day.

The Guildford Monarch, one of the many live-aboard canal boats on the Thames. — Photo by Gail Keck

Self-drive cruising on the River Thames

RANDY KECK, Contributing Editor

On a late-summer '94 trip to England to visit friends, courtesy of a large accumulation of frequent-flyer miles, I quite by accident happened on the perfect way to spend a sunny London day. This presumes, of course, that you can find one.

While exploring on foot near Windsor Castle, I noticed what appeared to be the odd rental boat in the River Thames. Since it was one of those rare occasions when we were not on a tight schedule, I decided to investigate. A few inquiries finally led us to the waterfront and Kris Cruisers, Southlea Road, Datchet, not far from Windsor.

At Kris Cruisers we discovered a small marina equipped with boats for both self-drive boating holidays and day-boat hire.

Our interest was in a day-boat hire and we selected one in the midsize "Royal Lady" category, licensed to carry eight passengers. This would prove to be more than ample for our group of four.

The main attraction, I must admit, was the opportunity we would have to pass through a number of locks on our half-day journey. I have always been fascinated by locks, in some sort of unexplainable way, and my opportunity to indulge this fascination was finally at hand.

Friendly encounters

The aura of the river at once prevailed, transforming our mood to a realm of peace and tranquillity. We were in the middle of a huge city, yet the river seemed to make the city disappear.

With picnic lunch aboard, we first traveled upstream, visiting Royal Windsor and, on the opposite bank, Eton, followed by the charming village of Bray. Farther on we arrived at Maidenhead with its history of Edwardian punting heydays.

All along the way, both upstream and downstream, we encountered live-aboard canal boats and barges. Some were for hire and many others served as second or permanent Thames-style homes of choice for fortunate Londoners.

We were most impressed by the genuine courtesy and friendliness expressed by all along the river.

Our trip downstream included historic Runnymede with its many heritage associations and the site where in 1215 King John affixed his seal to the Magna Carta.

The river winds on toward Staines, passing the London Stone, site of the former limit of jurisdiction of the City of London, and continuing on to Laleham, where riverside homes and bungalows gracefully front the meadows which once surrounded Laleham Abbey.

We chose one of numerous ideal moorings for our picnic lunch but just as easily could have tied up at one of the many riverside restaurants and pubs along the way.

Guided through

Ah, yes, the locks! These are not a problem, even for the uninitiated river boater, as all are operated by navigation staff ready to help and advise concerning any questions about a boater's journey. Our brief lock stops actually proved to be opportunities to meet and chat with other boating folk to exchange news and views on what lay ahead.

If it's your first time operating a boat, the Kris Cruisers staff will show you the controls, explain operating procedures and take you on a trial run. You also will be informed about the rules of navigation.

All locks on the Thames are controlled by staff of the National Rivers Authority, Thames Region. Lockkeepers will call you forward into each lock, take your lines and generally guide you through.

Boat hires

While our time allowed for only a day's outing, Kris Cruisers operates one of the largest fleets of fully equipped luxury cruisers on the River Thames. Boats have from two to 11 berths and are available for hire periods of a week or more.

With a cruiser, it is possible to explore the entire 124-mile length of the River Thames from Teddington right up to Lechlade in Gloucestershire. If you wish to hire a day boat for weekends and holidays, it is advisable to book in advance.

Our "Royal Lady" category 8-passenger cruiser was US$75 for a half day (four hours) and $140 for a full day (9 a.m. to 5:30 p.m.). These rates applied throughout the season, April through October. A 20% discount is in effect on weekday rentals, Monday through Friday.

For bookings and information, contact Kris Cruisers at The Waterfront, Southlea Road, Datchet, Berkshire SL3 9BU England; phone (0753) 543930.

Two small London Museums

HARRIET BRENNER, Kiawah Island, SC

My husband and I enjoyed visiting two small museums in London in the spring of '94.

• The Museum of London (150 London Wall, EC 2) can be reached by taking the Underground to St. Paul's station or Barbican station.

This compact museum illustrates the history and topography of London from prehistoric times to the present day. All the exhibits are arranged in chronological order and there are several full-size reconstructions and audiovisual displays, as well as models (e.g., a Roman waterfront).

This is not a museum that presents history behind glass; rather, it is a living chronicle of one of the world's greatest cities. It is even good for children, as the exhibits will appeal to all the senses. (They can participate in the Great Fire of London in living color and sound!)

Visitors can view the Lord Mayor's 3-ton state coach along with mock prison cells and shop counters from days past with authentic items. As an Anglophile, I found it fascinating.

The museum was opened in 1976 and there is a small restaurant. The admission charge was about US$4.50 for adults. It is closed on Monday.

• The other museum is the Museum of the Moving Image (MOMI), located at the South Bank Arts Center, Waterloo, London.

This museum presents a very complete history of the cinema and television through hands-on exhibits. Visitors can read the news on TV, animate their own cartoons, audition for a Hollywood movie or view the history of cinematic technology.

There are 72 laser players for video, as well as special screens and 3-D projections.

The collection of memorabilia includes costumes, Charlie Chaplin's cane and hat, Fred Astaire's tailcoat and vintage television sets. The museum employs several actor/guides to assist guests.

My husband and I are movie buffs and found this museum extremely interesting and unique. We never saw a compilation anywhere as complete as this. We spent over four hours there.

There is an interesting shop as well. The museum is closed Mondays.

Lodgings in London — short lets best bet

DICK LEE, Marina del Rey, CA

We've had many trips to London starting from '74, and we've learned a lot about lodgings, but for the most value at a moderate cost we think "short lets" are the best bet.

We found out about short lets a few years ago. All apartments in London are leased (a lease is called a let) and generally by the year or longer. However, a few owners or agents (called estate agents) will lease apartments for as little as one or two weeks; these are called short lets.

Let me tell you why we think they are better than B&Bs or hotels.

Weighing the alternatives

When we first went to London, we stayed at bed-and-breakfasts, typically by the British Museum; we'd get one room, either with a bathroom down the hall or a bathroom en suite.

Later, we just got the first night from the Victoria booking hall and then checked the "adverts."

One time, in addition to May and me, there were her two sons plus the wife of one — a total of five adults. May checked the *Evening Standard* newspaper and found a flat at Knightsbridge, right by Hyde Park. We had three bedrooms and a big, sunny living room. We'd meet at 5 p.m. for drinks, then plan our evening. We had a great time.

I forgot the price, but it was far better than a hotel or a B&B.

Of course, for a few nights a hotel or B&B is okay, but if you'll be there a week or more the space of an apartment is great. It will have a living room and a kitchen. You can then stock the kitchen and have your cereal and coffee in the morning, and your newsdealer (they are everywhere) will leave the *Times* in front of your door, just in time for your breakfast. Also, you can have friends over.

A favorite

In later years we found one of our favorites, **The Arlington**. It's on the side street of the **Ritz Hotel**. Though the flats are mostly privately owned, there are perhaps 20 or so available for short lets. (Lupis Property Co., 25 Arlington House; phone 171/629 0021 or fax 071/823-9244.)

The manager prefers to rent by the month, but a stop of two weeks is quite doable. We've stayed there for as little as one week, and they often can handle an odd number of days, like 10 days or 17 days, based on future bookings.

The flats are all complete with one or two bedrooms, a kitchen and an excellent living room. The kitchen is fully equipped and the crystal is Waterford. As of the fall of '96, the rate was about £560 per week or £80 ($130) per night — cheaper than many hotels. (In this article, I'm using $1.62 per pound.)

The location of the Arlington is superb, right at the Underground at Green Park, with buses on Piccadilly. And there always are cabs at the adjacent Ritz.

Our local restaurant is *Franco's Restaurant* at 63 Jermyn Street in St. James (phone 171 493 3645) — a good value and not very expensive.

Farther afield?

In the early '90s we were on a budget and sought less expensive lodgings — but still an apartment.

We found a private mews, near Swiss Cottage, north of London. It had three bedrooms, with living room and kitchen. It was very cozy, available when the owner was out of town, and the price was right, about £350 per week ($567 per week, or $81 per night). The owner would pick us up at Heathrow, and he would nicely stock the fridge.

In October '96 we stayed at a flat near West Hampstead, also north of London, at £370 ($599). The price was fine, and the cost of food was less since we could make some meals.

But it turned out that this flat was too far away; we had to take a bus to the Underground station, then the Underground to central London. The flat was cheap, but the dilemma was that if I were on business in London in the afternoon and wanted to attend a play in the evening, we had to pass three to four hours going back and forth.

In the future, we'll take short lets closer to the center of London, i.e., Mayfair, Knightsbridge, Kensington, South Kensington, Sloane Square, Bloomsbury, Marble Arch and the like.

London economics 101

As to the economics, there are only about three alternatives: hotels, B&Bs and short lets. I suspect there are hotels at less than £100, but a decent one is from £100 to £150 and more daily (and they can easily get to £200-£300 per day).

The rooms are fine, but if you want food you must get dressed to go out of the room to the hotel restaurant or outside to one on the street. Per week, at £150 per day, the hotel costs £1,050 ($1,700).

The B&Bs are a lot less than the hotels, but, as with the hotels, if you want to eat dinner you'll have to go out and pay retail.

The short lets are the best for several reasons. First, there are more rooms. Besides the bedrooms and the bathrooms you have a kitchen and a living room. You can get what you want from the local market, and by late afternoon you can get drinks and fix a real meal. And breakfast is easy, quick and cheap.

If you will be doing some business, you need the access of a telephone — this is no problem with a hotel, of course, but difficult at a B&B. But I'm happy to say that BT (the local telephone in London) offers Call Minder at the flat, at the moderate rate of £4.50 ($7.29) per quarter. It takes a message when you're out and even while you're using the phone. Nifty.

Now, go for it

If you're already in London, the best newspaper I've found is the *Evening Standard*. It lists lets in all of the London vicinities and also the suburbs.

The price is always quoted by the week, even though they will lease it for a year or more; you just must phone a lot. Also, estate agents show availability. If an estate agent does not handle short lets, ask if she or he can recommend anyone who will.

Hub city makes it easy to explore using public transport

SHARON L. NEESE, Indianapolis, IN

Having accumulated sufficient air miles for two tickets to Europe, the questions now were where and when to go and also whether to use public transportation or rent a car, for this determined the type of trip we would plan.

We decided to go for two weeks in the latter part of April 1996. Public transportation seemed best for this trip and, because we did not wish to continually be moving our luggage, two "hub" cities were selected: London and, as this should have been the "blooming season," Amsterdam.

B&B arrangements

As we spend a minimum amount of time in the room when on a vacation, we choose to stay in bed-and-breakfasts with a shared bath. When we arrived in London, we obtained our room at the hotel/B&B desk at the airport.

The room was nothing to write home about, but it was relatively clean, inexpensive for London and in the Victoria area, which was truly convenient for train, Tube and bus.

London hub

London: why was that one of our destination choices?

We enjoy taking in a show or two and shopping. In fact, we visited our favorite London stores and shopping areas two of the four days.

At Hampton Court Palace, guides in period costume help bring to life the times of King Henry VIII.

On one of the remaining two days we visited Hampton Court Palace. One of the brochures calls it "Britain's Most Beautiful Time Capsule," and that it is! Costumed guides will take you on tours of various apartments or areas, or you may use the headsets for tape-recorded tours. There is no extra charge for either type of tour and they also have special events throughout the day.

One tour that we took was through the beautifully restored gardens. They were formally re-opened in July 1995. Our guide for this tour was the "Keeper of the Vine," whose main job it is to care for the venerable and beloved grape vine.

Although Hampton Court is a distance from the center of London, it may be reached by Tube and bus, and a London day transportation card covers the entire trip.

On our last day in London we took the train to Canterbury. We had not been in this part of England before and it was nice to visit the cathedral and take the town tour.

New British Library

LLOYD McCUNE, Contributing Editor

The new British Library, nicknamed "the Great British Disaster" opened on schedule on Nov. 24, '97, more than 30 years following its initial planning. Its total cost has amounted to 9510 million!

A massive red building next to St. Pancras station in north London, its construction has been interrupted more than once due to lack of funds.

The library, which contains some 10 million books, will not be fully functional until 1999. Many of the books found here are from the old British Library, which had been housed in the British Museum since 1857.

The National Heritage Committee joined other sources in condemning this new building, but perhaps the patina of time will make it less offensive.

As the old Austrian emperor Franz Joseph once said, when asked his opinion of a new construction in Vienna, "*Lassen wir es iiberwachsen*" (very rough translation: "Let's let time work on it").

Many of the Victorian and later art nouveau creations that were at one time reviled and ridiculed have become treasured collectors' items sometimes worth more than their original value.

A short train-hop away from our suburban London apartment was the suburban London residence of King Henry VIII, Hampton Court Palace. The Clock Court displays an astronomical clock made for the king. Anne Boleyn's Gateway is found here; today, it's the gathering place for the guided tours of the palace.

Outer London — A great place to stay — and fun to explore

LEI CHATFIELD, Senior Editor, ITN

A 10-day trip to London, from California, for less than it would cost for a week's package to Branson, Missouri? We did just that by using a low-season airfare and staying in a comfortable apartment — in quiet and safe suburban London.

Best of both worlds

Outer London, including Wimbledon, Hampton Court, Greenwich. . . I already had found this city fringe area to be rich in historical sights — the perfect escape from the intensity (wonderful though it is) of London.

On our February visit my husband, daughter and I also found it to be an escape from the high prices of lodging there, yet we were only 30 minutes from Victoria Station, the heart of London activity. We took advantage of the best of both worlds.

Notice the Tudor chimneys in the background. William and Mary later built a classical-style wing onto the Tudor Hampton Court.

Although public-transport passes, pub grub and half-price theater tickets entered into keeping costs down, the major savings came from our $400-each tickets on British Airways and the suburban apartment rental in Raynes Park, just one BritRail stop after the Wimbledon Tube station.

Commuting each day, I began to see familiar faces. . . and felt more a part of London than when I had stayed in the city itself.

Intriguing Hampton Court

The first-time traveler to London is hard-pressed enough for time just to see the major attractions of the city: the Tower of London, British Museum, Buckingham Palace, Westminster Abbey, etc.

We invariably return to these, but some of the greatest treasures are beyond the city, such as Hampton Court Palace, King Henry VIII's abode, just a short train-hop away from our accommodations at Raynes Park.

Hampton Court was a special treat for our daughter, Kim, as she's fascinated by the King Henry VIII, Tudor period of history. (If you are, too, be sure to go to London's Madame Tussaud's museum with its wonderful wax figures of Henry and his six wives.)

At Hampton Court Palace, built in the 16th century by Cardinal Wolsey and given over as a "gift" to Henry, visitors can't help but get the true feel of royal life, with all its intrigues, in those times. I would suggest allotting a full day there.

Once the general admission is paid, all tours are gratis, so it's just a matter of timing yourself for a walk with a costumed guide into the time of Henry and, later, William and Mary.

The palace, under the reign of William and Mary, took on a new look, Baroque and classical, with the architect Christopher Wren; this is quite apparent in the East Wing. The entire Tudor wing would have gone the same way, but the budget — thankfully — ran out; thus, we have a wonderful example of Tudor architecture left.

We spent the whole day there and missed three of the tours, but we wanted enough time to explore the extensive Tudor, Baroque and Victorian gardens.

Kim loved getting lost and finally finding her way out of the maze — a Tudor legacy, of course.

If you have limited time, I'd suggest touring the Tudor royal lodgings; the guides will make the intricacies of court life come alive.

For example, beyond the Tudor Great Hall, with its fantastic ceiling and stained-glass windows, is the Haunted Gallery.

It was there that Henry VIII's fifth wife, Catherine Howard, was apprehended as she ran down the hall to plead to the king to spare her life. She was stopped short of reaching him at the Chapel Royal — and ultimately suffered the same fate as her cousin, Anne Boleyn.

It is said she haunts the gallery to this day.

A not-to-be-missed tour is that of the Tudor kitchens, the best 16th-century kitchens anywhere. There are free headsets available to guide you and explain the goings on of the kitchens which are all set for a Tudor feast. (Note the huge, open-fire rotisserie, which ran by weights — no man-power needed.)

Modern-day visitors may get hungry at this point, but there's no need to leave Hampton Court; there's a restaurant and a cafeteria available. We opted for the cafeteria, which takes less time, and were pleased with the hearty fare and reasonable prices.

We chose to visit Hampton Court on a Sunday because most of London closes down, including most theaters. This is an important consideration in planning your time.

Considering that, and following the King Henry theme, let's move on to another outer London destination: Greenwich.

Maritime Greenwich

This maritime setting is quite significant, given the power of England as a seafaring nation. It was here that Henry, and his daughters, Elizabeth I and Mary Tudor, were born. It was under Henry that the navy became a permanent force.

The palace in which the royals were born is long gone, but now you can see Inigo Jones' Queen's House instead. Designed in the Italian Palladian style, its outstanding feature is its "tulip staircase" named for the wrought-iron design on its balustrades; it was also the first cantilevered staircase in England.

The view from the Queen's House balcony is the same today as in the 17th century: the Thames is seen in all its glory because the Royal Naval College was built in two halves so as not to obstruct the view.

Of course, Greenwich has much more to offer: the weekend craft and antique market, the National Maritime Museum, the *Gipsy Moth IV* and *Cutty Sark* sailing vessels. . . And, at the Old Royal Observatory, where the world's mean time is measured, you can straddle the meridian line.

Looking from the extensive formal gardens of Hampton Court toward the east wing of the palace, extended in the 1690s by William and Mary and designed by Sir Christopher Wren.

A few London notes

Volumes have been written about London itself — I discover more on each visit. I just want to interject some money-saving tips.

When exchanging money, if you have a Citibank credit card, go to a Citibank branch office; the one near Covent Garden charged us no commission when exchanging money, upon the presentation of my card.

If you enjoy the theater, you can go at half price; check to see what's available at the ticket booth at Leicester Square (near the Tube stop of the same name). It's a first-come, first-served situation and only on the day of performance. But we got front-row seats for "Blood Brothers" at half price — one of the best plays I've seen. Cost was £13.75 plus £2 service charge, or about $25 total, per ticket.

Also, don't be discouraged by "sellout" plays. We got tickets to "Miss Saigon" on the day of performance at the box office in the historic Theatre Royal Drury Lane — at a discounted price. We also took the backstage tour at £4 each; it was well worth it.

The eating places in the theater district offer some good values. Shop around; they post their menus.

Specifics

Upon arrival in London at Heathrow, we each got a London Transport Travelcard good in Zones 1 through 4, which includes the inner suburbs. It gave us access to the inner-city trains, subway network, Docklands Light Rail and buses.

All you need is an I.D. photo; machines are available in the terminal.

As for the apartments, I highly recommend Big Ben Apartment Rentals which has apartments in Central London areas such as Victoria, Kensington and Earls Court.

Personally, I enjoyed the "select suburbs" approach. Apartments are available in Richmond, Putney, Highgate, Hampstead, Oakwood and Southgate.

The minimum stay generally is seven nights, but sometimes it's possible to get a last-minute booking of up to three nights to fill a gap. On average, bookings are made three to six months ahead; some people book nine months ahead to ensure a certain location.

There always is someone from Big Ben on hand to greet guests and orient them regarding the apartment, getting around, etc.

If you want to go farther afield, the company also has a B&B available in the resort of Eastbourne, located near the seafront and offering a base for visiting the surrounding Sussex countryside. A rarity for England, the B&B is nonsmoking.

For more details, contact Big Ben Apartment Rentals, P.O. Box 2612, Eastbourne BN20 7PW, England; phone/fax 011 44 1323 - 728494.

The Duke of Kent and Charlton Heston greet a WWII veteran.

Journey to Duxford — Britain remembers WWII Americans with new museum

ROCHELLE OLDFIELD, Walnut Creek, CA

My husband's father passed away last year. While going through his papers, we found that he had contributed to a museum that was being built in England.

I was curious and wrote several letters. I learned that the museum was almost complete. It was located at Duxford just outside of Cambridge and was dedicated to the Americans who flew out of Great Britain during World War II.

Cause and effect

My husband's father had been a fighter pilot during the war and had been shot down over Holland. He spent time with the Dutch underground and had been there for the liberation of Paris.

Most British military museums focus on individual soldiers. I knew that my husband's father would love to have his story remembered.

I suggested that we contribute his collection of old photos, his medals and his story to the museum. My husband agreed. We packed up everything and shipped it off UPS.

Several months passed and I had completely forgotten about Duxford.

One day the mail arrived with a

letter from Great Britain. It contained an invitation from Field Marshal Lord Bramall on behalf of Her Majesty the Queen. We had been invited to attend the opening of the American Air Museum at Duxford; the Queen would preside over the ceremony.

I wasn't going to let an opportunity like this slip by. I immediately booked airline and hotel reservations through British Airways.

Then I called my husband and told him that we were going.

Take your umbrella

On the morning of July 31, 1997, we purchased two train tickets to Cambridge at the King's Cross station in London and miraculously found the right train just before it was due to depart.

The one-hour journey took us through London and into the English countryside.

All of my prior trips to England had been in the winter. I was surprised to see the pastureland filled with wildflowers, fat magpies and freshly sheared sheep. I wished that we had more time so that I could get off the train and enjoy the English summer.

We arrived in Cambridge and took a taxi to the **Gonville Hotel**. It was too early to check in and it was raining and we did not have umbrellas. I didn't know what to do.

The porter suggested that we

A rainy day in Cambridge.

walk through the town. He loaned us two umbrellas and commented, "You should know that no one comes to England without an umbrella."

The historic Eagle

We spent the rest of the day enjoying old Cambridge. The famous university was only 10 minutes away. Most of the buildings date from the Middle Ages.

I knew that the library housed a collection of works by one of my favorite authors, the 19th-century traveler Sir Richard Burton, and was open to the public for a small fee. I was tempted to go in, but there was something else that I wanted to do first.

My husband's father used to tell us stories about a pub that was popular with the pilots during the war. I thought that its name was *The Eagle*. It was close to lunchtime and most pubs serve food, so I asked a clerk at the British Teddy Bear Company (a shop that sells only teddies) if The Eagle still existed.

She said, "Of course; it's just around the corner on Benet Street."

We found The Eagle and went in. It was lunchtime, but it was not crowded. I asked the bartender if food was available and he pointed us through a series of wood-paneled rooms to the back of the building where we could order.

The Eagle has smoking and nonsmoking sections and an outdoor courtyard. Like most English pubs, it has numerous rooms and more than one bar. It turned out that we were early; shortly after we arrived every seat was taken.

I had excellent fish and chips and a half pint of Old Goat ale. My husband had his usual pint of lager.

After lunch I asked the bartender about the place. He told us that it had been popular with pilots during World War II and that there was a bar in the back where they had written the names of their squadrons on the ceiling with candle smoke.

We went and looked into the Air Force Bar. Its paint yellowed with age, the ceiling was covered with names that were still legible. The walls were covered with photos from the war.

It gave me a chill to think that my husband's father may have stood on that very spot over 50 years ago.

Today The Eagle is popular with university students and professors. In fact, the two scientists who discovered DNA are said to have first discussed the matter here.

A punting we will go

In the afternoon we hired a boat (or punt) for a guided tour of the river Cam. The river flows by the university and provides an excellent way to see Cambridge's famous gardens (the College "Backs") and bridges.

Our guide was a university student; he must remain nameless because students at Cambridge are not supposed to work. They are expected to devote all their time to study. The price that day was negotiable because business was slow.

That evening we went back to The Eagle. There was a group of old pilots having a party in the Air Force Bar. We went in and introduced ourselves. Like us, they

The "Eagle" pub in Cambridge was popular with pilots during WWII. Today it is popular with university students and professors.

were there for the museum opening. We asked if any of them had known my husband's father, but no one recalled the name. They were all bomber pilots.

We asked the bartender if he could recommend a good restaurant. He directed us to a place on Trumpington Street. As we walked, I noticed that the gutters on either side of the road flowed with water.

I later learned that these were the rivers Pem and Pot. Thomas Hobson (known for the expression "Hobson's choice") had diverted a creek into the gutters in order to provide running water for the town. These "channels" date back to 1610.

We had dinner at *Browns*, a lively place popular with locals. It serves English specialties and pasta. Reservations are not needed.

The big day

The next day we took a taxi to Duxford, about a 10-mile trip. One may also travel to Duxford by train (get off at Wittleford Station); the cost is about half the cost of a taxi.

This was the big day. The American Air Museum would open in the afternoon following its dedication by the Queen. The museum is part of the Imperial War Museum at Duxford. We spent much of the morning viewing its exhibits of aircraft.

Unfortunately, it started to rain again. We headed for a hangar that had been set up to provide luncheon and bar service for the invited guests.

I was enjoying a cup of tea when I suddenly realized that I was standing next to the Duke of Kent and the actor Charlton Heston. I almost dropped my cup. Mr. Heston had been involved in fund raising for the museum in America and the Duke of Kent was a museum sponsor.

It eventually stopped raining. Everyone headed outside to find a dry seat for the ceremony. The crowd was filled with veterans. Many were in the uniforms that they had worn during the war.

The Queen's plane arrived in the early afternoon; she had a private tour of the facility. There was a series of short speeches by the Queen, Charlton Heston and other notables, then a fly-past of vintage aircraft and finally the museum was opened.

The exhibits

The museum is an impressive structure of concrete and glass in the form of a half dome. It appears as a bunker designed to protect aircraft from enemy attack.

The interior consists of one vast room filled with American warplanes that date from World War I to the current day. The exhibits are all beautifully restored.

I was impressed with the B-25 and B-29 bombers from the World War II era. The size of the museum is demonstrated by the fact that it holds a complete B-52 bomber (still in service today).

Although the museum does not contain historically significant aircraft, such as our own Smithsonian, it is every bit as impressive.

We eventually found ourselves in a small alcove dedicated to the American pilots who had flown out of England during World War II.

The walls at either end of the room are black marble. The name of each American flyer who lost his life during the war is engraved in an honor role there.

The center wall contains a glass display case with exhibits. I looked in and there was a picture of Lt. Charles S. Oldfield along with his military medals and his story of evading capture.

I knew that he would be happy to be in such a fine place.

If you go

British Airways provides daily nonstop service from San Francisco International Airport to London.

Frequent trains run daily from King's Cross station in London to Cambridge.

If you drive, take the M2 Motorway. Driving time from London is about one hour.

The American Air Museum is located about eight miles away from Cambridge. It is next to junction 10 of the M2 Motorway.

For more information on public transportation, call 01223-835000.

We stayed at the **Gonville Hotel**, a Best Western International Hotel. It is a 3-star hotel and features a full English breakfast and many amenities. It is located a short 10-minute walk from the historic university.

Reservations can be made through their toll-free number: 800/233-1234.

To contact the American Air Museum, call 800/233-4226 or 202/543-4226.

For further information on England, you can call the British Tourist Authority at 800/462-2748.

England

Polperro, a former smugglers' haven on the Cornish coast, is now a mecca for tourists.

Quaint villages to wild coastal beauty — Devon and Cornwall have it all

JUDY NIEMANN, San Angelo, TX

When our young English friends Caroline and Graham Richards learned we'd be driving through Devon and Cornwall on our next trip to England, they asked if we'd like company.

We'd still have to rent a car, as theirs wasn't suitable, but Graham would drive and we'd share the cost of gasoline. Don could sit back and enjoy the scenery instead of concentrating on "keeping left" as he'd done during our two years in England with the U.S. Air Force and on subsequent driving vacations in England and Ireland.

First stop, London

We arrived at Gatwick on a nonstop American Airlines flight from Dallas early on Oct. 21, 1997. We like Gatwick because we can check in at Victoria Station for our return flight and have the airline transport our checked bags to the airport, leaving us only our carry-on bags to handle on the half-hour train ride to the terminal.

My first stop at any foreign destination is the automatic teller machine (ATM) to withdraw from my checking account back home a

---

***Preceeding page: A man herds his sheep to pasture near Wigglesworth.** — Photo by Rochelle Oldfield, Walnut Creek, CA*

---

few hundred dollars in local currency. Our initial expense was two one-way tickets on the *Gatwick Express* to Victoria (£15/$25).

We spent our first two nights in a small but newly decorated room at **Tophams Ebury Court Hotel** (£230/$382, including full English breakfast ordered from the menu). Just 3½ blocks from Victoria Station, the Ebury is an easy walk with wheeled luggage.

Caroline and a colleague, in London for a trade show, drove us to her home in a small village in Cambridgeshire for a 2-day stay.

Slow road to Falmouth

Saturday, we loaded the car and headed for Falmouth, on the east coast of Cornwall, along with everyone else in England, or so it seemed. The bumper-to-bumper traffic was moving at a snail's pace when we reached the M5 north of Bristol. We never learned if an auto accident or roadwork caused the delay, but it took over an hour to travel the last 14 miles to Bristol.

Hoping traffic would clear while we ate, we lunched at *McDonald's* just off the motorway in Bristol, but it was nearly two more hours before we could resume a normal speed. Night had fallen before we reached the **Falmouth Beach Hotel**, where Caroline had booked us.

Though a bit crowded, our room had a king-size bed, two lounge chairs, television with remote control, tea- and coffee-making facilities and a balcony with a view of the beach. Our package cost £360/$605 for four nights, including breakfast and dinner, both buffet style, and use of the neighboring hotel's gymnasium.

The Lizard Peninsula

Don and I arose early each morning and walked through the garden to exercise next door before meeting our friends for a hearty English breakfast.

We left shortly after 9 a.m. to explore the Cornish coast with Graham at the wheel and Caroline navigating, following an itinerary they had put together. On the narrow roads, Graham frequently had to back up until he found a spot wide enough for an oncoming car to pass.

The first day, we explored the Lizard Peninsula, the southeastern corner of Cornwall. As we visited numerous villages and coastal coves, I thought of Daphne du Maurier's "Frenchman's Creek" and searched in vain for ghostly smugglers' ships.

In the fishing village of Cadgwith, Don and I tasted our first Cornish pasties, the traditional "sandwich meal" which tin miners carried in their shirt pockets instead of lunch buckets, and shared our lunch with the resident dog.

We continued to Lizard Point, England's southernmost spot, where we laughed as flying seagulls stalled against the strong coastal winds.

At Kynance Cove the long, steep path was difficult for my arthritic knees, but the wild beauty of the cliffs and rocky shore made it worth the effort. At Mullion Cove, we walked on the jetty and watched an artist capture the scene on canvas.

In our hotel dining room that evening, many of the English women line-danced to the live country western music, but I could only watch, never having learned the intricate steps.

St. Michael's Mount

The next day we explored the shops of Falmouth, purchasing prints by one of Caroline and Graham's favorite artists, and strolled the sandy beach at Praa Sands before heading for Marazion and one of my must-see sites, St. Michael's Mount.

Cornish pasty shop in St. Ives, Cornwall.

We walked along the stone causeway from shore when, before I could climb up to join the others at the boat landing, the incoming tide broke over the causeway steps — and me. I got drenched even more as the prow of the small boat that ferried us across the water dipped into each wave.

The castle atop the mount still serves as a private home but is now a National Trust property with much of the building and grounds open to the public. My knees got another good workout climbing the steep path and countless steps.

When we left the mount, the causeway was completely under water. Our boat, its waterproof covering now drawn up to shelter us from the waves, dropped us on shore.

To Land's End

In Mousehole, Don tried his first chip butty. I had already tasted one on an earlier visit to England, but we all joined him in this unusual sandwich of chips (French fries) between two pieces of white bread. I've heard that it originated during the meat shortage in World War II England.

Next we drove to Land's End, another "must see." Don and I had once visited John O'Groats in northeastern Scotland and I was determined to see its opposite point in southwestern England.

Caroline had warned me the area now has an amusement park atmosphere, but I was still enthralled by its wild beauty as we battled the fierce winds to keep our footing.

Cornwall's west coast

On our final full day in Cornwall we covered the west coast from St. Ives to Newquay. When we arrived in St. Ives, the tide was out, leaving the boats in the harbor high and dry, but the sandy beach served as a launching pad for one kite flyer whose wind-filled kite occasionally lifted him into the air.

Little remains of Cornwall's tin mines, but Caroline and Graham wanted us to see the skeletons of the Wheal Coates mine above the coast near St. Agnes. As the sun dropped lower in the west, we visited Newquay and the Bedruthan Steps.

Polperro

The next morning we checked out of the hotel, fueled the car and headed for Cornwall's historic fishing village of Polperro, a former smugglers' haven and now a tourist mecca.

You can ride into town from the car park in a horse-drawn carriage or small double-decker bus, or walk the short distance alongside a cool stream and whitewashed cottages. At the *House on Props* we ate a traditional ploughman's lunch, a bit pricey at £18.30/$30.50 for four, including beverages.

On to Devon

In Devon we stayed in Goodrington in a 2-bedroom holiday flat owned by Caroline's cousin. The cost of £25/$42 for two nights' accommodation did not include linens, but Caroline had brought them along.

Our first priority was rounding up enough 50p and £1 coins to keep the electric and gas meters running during our occupancy. When Graham dismantled an extra bed in one of the bedrooms, we discovered several coins on the floor, one of which was an all-important older 50p piece. The size of this denomination has changed and only the older, larger coin works in the meter.

That evening in Torquay, Caroline and Graham ordered a delicious East Indian meal with numerous interesting accompaniments.

Don and I walked about three blocks to the beach on our first morning in Devon. Even at 7 a.m. we were greeted by many people walking their dogs.

Dartmouth excursion

After a breakfast of tea, toast, canned fruit and cereal from provisions Caroline and Graham had purchased nearby, we drove to neighboring Paignton where Don and I boarded an old-time steam train for the 7-mile, 30-minute ride to Kingswear. Caroline and Graham drove ahead and were already in line for the car ferry to Dartmouth when our train chugged into the station.

Our primary destination was Slapton Sands, where a Sherman tank memorializes approximately 1,000 Americans who were killed, wounded or lost at sea during Operation Tiger, part of the D-Day landing rehearsal.

The American government erected an obelisk elsewhere on the beach in tribute to the thousands of local residents who temporarily evacuated their homes and farms during the exercises.

Most days, you can meet Englishman Ken Small, who fought for 13 years to rescue the tank, also a casualty of the training, from its watery grave and convince the American government to recognize it as a memorial. He chronicled his struggle in a book, "The Forgotten Dead," which he sells to interested visitors from the trunk of his car.

After a tour of Dartmouth Castle and a return ferry ride across the River Dart, we watched night fall and the lights flicker on the water as we strolled around Brixham. Later we traveled along dark, narrow country roads bordered by tall hedgerows to the *Old Bickley Inn* for dinner.

Winding down

Friday morning, after eating and packing the car, the four of us took a final walk along the beach, tossing scraps of leftover bread to the feathered beggars we encountered. But before heading for London, where Graham and Caroline were dropping us, we still had a lot of Devon to see.

We returned to Brixham to see this Mediterranean-look village by daylight and to shop for artwork, then drove up the hill from the harbor to Berry Head, a grass-covered promontory with a panoramic view of the sea.

Driving through Dartmoor National Park, we spotted an occasional wild pony and saw several more ambling around the village green in picturesque Widecombe-in-the-Moor, a hamlet dwarfed by its medieval church's tower.

We stopped at the top of the moor for an in-car picnic lunch of Cornish pasties, a sausage roll (my favorite English snack), Eccles cakes and bottled water we had purchased in Brixham.

Alas, it was time to head for London. Undaunted by the Friday night crowds, Graham patiently maneuvered our car through Piccadilly Circus and Trafalgar Square to the **St. James Court Hotel**, where we bid our friends farewell.

The St. James (£587/$975 for four nights) provided a luxurious finale to our trip and was a short taxi ride (£3.40/$5.65 plus tip) from Victoria Station and our American Airlines check-in.

Our Budget rental car cost £179/$295 for eight days. Although we made 30 miles per American gallon, we spent over $50 every time we filled the tank at nearly $1.08 per liter.

Judy, Graham and Caroline as they begin their tour of the coast of Cornwall.

St. Michael's Mount in Penzance is reachable by a causeway at low tide, but the trip must be made by boat when the tides are in.

Lured to Cornwall by sister-city duo

BOB RICHELSON, Penn Valley, CA

One hundred and fifty years ago there was a mass exodus of tin miners from Cornwall, the westernmost county of England, to Northern California's Mother Lode country. The lure was gold.

A reenactment of that original journey is expected from now until the millennium and beyond. Only this time it will be 2-directional. Much of it will involve residents of the Cornish towns of Bodmin and Penzance and their Mother Lode sister cities, Grass Valley and Nevada City.

The latter are key players in the California Sesquicentennial, a 3-year event marking the 150th anniversaries of the discovery of gold (1848-1998), the Gold Rush (1849-1999) and California statehood (1850-2000).

Many Cornish descendants from other parts of the U.S. and Canada will participate in the Grass Valley-Nevada City festivities. Others will return to the homeland of their ancestors. Still others will do both.

Off to Cornwall

Having heard glowing reports of a recent journey to Cornwall made by a local contingent, we decided to include it on the itinerary for our latest flight to England.

From London, and following local advice, we booked seats on the Paddington-to-Penzance train, disembarking at Truro to pick up a rental car to complete the 30-mile trip to Penzance. Truro is the administrative center of Cornwall, which has a total population of just under a half million.

The county's mild climate and scenic beauty — the rocky cliffs, lush green fields, windswept moorlands and fine beaches and harbors — have made it a favorite with vacationers.

"Pirates of Penzance"

Penzance (population 19,000) gained international fame with Gilbert and Sullivan's comic opera "Pirates of Penzance." Today its leading tourist attraction is St. Michael's Mount, a sometimes island that's a smaller version of Normandy's Mont St. Michel. Both date back to the 12th century.

Some 3,000 people tour St. Michael's on a typical summer day. At low tide it's accessible by a causeway. When the tides roll in, the trip must be made by boat.

Those making the ascent to the castle should be in good health and wear durable, slip-retardant footwear. Others can browse the gift shop and other ground-level structures.

In Penzance we stayed at the traditionally English **Queen's Hotel** overlooking Mount's Bay. Room rates include a full breakfast. Many paintings from the Newlyn Orion Gallery are on display at the hotel.

A street scene in Bodmin, taken in front of Town Council offices.

The gallery, the Egyptian House, the nautical and maritime museums and Morrah Gardens are all worth seeing.

Beyond Penzance

From Penzance we drove north 10 miles to St. Ives on the west coast, where we found superb beaches, hardy, wet-suited surfers, palm trees and the Tate Gallery, featuring art from the 19th century on.

We then headed to enchanting and mysterious Land's End at the most southwestern tip of England. In addition to a spectacular view of an old lighthouse, it offers gift shops, dining and lodging facilities.

For those who want to go even farther west, there are the remote but scenic Isles of Scilly 30 miles distant.

They are reachable in 25 minutes by plane from Land's End (cost: $56 for adults). By boat, the journey from Penzance takes two hours, 40 minutes. The fare is $32, with an $8 discount for seniors on Mondays and Thursdays on advance reservations.

Road to Bodmin

The next day we motored north on the fast A30 some 40 miles to Bodmin, where one can see the remains of the monastery and priory that were part of the largest 15th-century parish church in Cornwall.

Bodmin Gaol, scene of many public executions in years gone by, is now a popular tourist attraction as is a steam railway on which one can wine and dine.

Other favored attractions are Lanhydrock, a 49-room estate house dating back to the 17th century; Pengarrow, a warm Georgian home with elegant gardens, and novelist Daphne du Maurier's *Jamaica Inn*. Other notables from the area are John Wesley, founder of Methodism, the county's predominant religion, and Richard Trevithick, inventor of the Cornish engine so vital to mining endeavors.

There are interesting parallels between Bodmin and Grass Valley. Each has good downtown parking, a downtown athletic field with stands, golf courses, vineyards, a downtown Safeway market and, of course, Cornish pasties, those tasty pastry shells filled with meat, potatoes, onions and parsley.

From Bodmin we drove to Lizard Peninsula, the most southerly part of England, where craggy cliffs overlook the English Channel. At Lizard Village, serpentine-rock gift shops are clustered around the village green and the lighthouse and lifeboat station are within easy walking distance.

Some matters to consider

If Cornwall is in your travel plans, there are some pecuniary and pronunciation matters to be considered.

After cashing in a frequent-flyer coupon, we saved some $400 on a companion ticket after checking prices for various dates.

Our Paddington-Penzance round trip cost about $100 each. Had we not juggled dates, we could have paid double that.

At each tourist attraction, look into discounts for seniors (old age pensioners).

As for pronunciations, Penzance, like Nevada City, calls for a broad-"a" second syllable (Penzaance, Ne-vaada). Mousehole, the quaint fishing village south of Penzance, is pronounced Mousel. The "c" in Scilly is silent, making them the Isles of Silly.

Cornwall has its own distinctive dialect. A native of Cornwall has difficulty understanding someone from such northern counties as Yorkshire and Northumberland.

A narrow ravine leading to the sea is called a *coomb* in Cornwall and Devon, a *cline* in Hampshire and a *dale* in Yorkshire.

For more info

For more information, contact the British Tourist Authority, 551 Fifth Ave., New York, NY 10176; phone 800/462-2748. . . British Rail, c/o Spring, O'Brien & Co., 50 W. 23rd St., New York, NY 10010; phone 212/620-7100 . . . Tourism & Public Relations Section, St. Clare, Penzance, Cornwall TR18 3QW, England. . . or Bodmin Tourist Information, Mount Folly Square, Bodmin, Cornwall PL31 2DQ, England.

Mysterious ruins of Tintagel Castle on the windswept northwest coast of Cornwall. Legend long associated King Arthur with Tintagel.

Springtime on the coast — a meander to the castles of Cornwall

Wm. TERRY SMITH, Fort Collins, CO

The congestion of London gave way to ever-smaller towns and finally to open countryside as we sped southwest on the M3. My wife and I had just finished a delightful spring stay in London, replete with marvelous theater, wonderful dining and the ever-present civility of this great city. Now, driving on the left side of the road in our rental car and with only a vague itinerary in mind, we were off to explore the mysteries of ancient Cornwall.

Jumping the gun

We soon exited the M3 onto Route A30. Having had our fill of high-speed travel, we were more than ready to slow things down to an amble.

Our first stop was a charming country pub called the *Monk Court Inn*, nestled in a tiny village just east of Honiton.

Technically, we were still in Devon, but we celebrated the approach of our destination with Cornish pasties — savory baked concoctions of vegetables, spices, cheeses and ground meats encased in piping-hot pie crusts. Every pub has its own version of this regional specialty, and we sampled more than our fair share over the next few days.

Castles and more

Our first castle loomed in the distance shortly after lunch as we approached Launceston.

Perched high on a grassy mound, it overlooks the town on one side and towers above sheep-filled meadows on the other. The innermost part of the castle, called the keep, dates to the 12th century. Other remains trace to the 13th century, and the impressive gate is of 14th-century vintage.

Like several other Norman castles in these parts, Launceston's distinguishing feature is its perfectly round shape.

Just down the road from Launceston is Bodmin Moor. It is everything a proper moor should be: a barren, rock-strewn landscape stretching out to infinity with only an occasional sprinkling of sheep to break the monotony.

But this moor has more. It was the one-time home of Daphne du Maurier and the setting for her famous novel "Jamaica Inn." It's touristy, but a wayside stop by the same name is worth a few minutes for those who loved the book.

Leaving Bodmin, we tracked and backtracked on country roads to the medieval town of Lostwithiel on the banks of the River Fowey. Our first order of business was finding lodging for the night. We checked out a couple of alternatives before settling on a family-run establishment on North Street called **The Globe Inn**. Our comfortable second-floor room featured a a wood-burning fireplace and a floor sloping from centuries of settling.

Dinner for two with wine in the pub below was simple but very tasty and a good value at $35.

Just north of Lostwithiel, on a tree-shrouded bend in the River Fowey, stands Restormel Castle. This charming Norman relic is in remarkably good condition and features beautiful views of the surrounding countryside.

As it was early April, daffodils bloomed in profusion in every direction. Adding to the overall effect was the fact that no one else was around; we were able to wander about and drink in the beauty at our leisure.

Coasting along

Cornwall's history is inexorably linked to the sea, so it was time to find our way to the coast the next morning. We chose Fowey on St. Austell Bay as our first port of call. Its former citizens include Iron Age inhabitants, Romans and a host of infamous pirates. The city survived in spite of periodic efforts by the French and Spanish to burn it to the ground.

What remains today is a maze of twisting streets that eventually deposit you at the waterfront. Small hotels, quaint restaurants and antique shops now occupy many of the medieval buildings. All in all, the ambience is delightful. To get an overall perspective of Fowey, take the short ferry ride across the harbor to Polruan, a pleasant village in its own right.

Knowing England's reputation for beautiful gardens, we decided to stop at Trewithen on the road from Fowey to Truro. What a find! The 30-acre estate is internationally known for its collection of camellias, rhododendrons and magnolias, and they were all in full bloom when we visited. The winding paths lead from one eye-pleasing setting to another. And because the crowds don't show up until summer, we had the place virtually to ourselves.

The foreboding ruins of Restormel Castle near Lostwithiel.

Late afternoon found us back on the coast in Falmouth. We couldn't take our eyes off the enchanting seascape, so we searched for a room with a view. We discovered it at a large vacation house on Emslie Road, now converted into a B&B called the **Chelsea House Hotel**. Our spacious en suite room was immaculate. It truly was an off-season bargain at $53.

Several seafood restaurants beckoned for our attention in the waterfront area. We feasted on lemon sole and fresh scallops at the *Seafood Bar* on Lower Quay Hill ($50 with wine).

Falmouth sports one of the most dramatic castles in all of Cornwall. Called Pendennis, it has guarded the sea approach to the city for more than 450 years (Henry VIII commissioned its construction). It is in mint condition and a pleasure to visit.

Of special interest is the wax-fashioned cannon crew on the upper level. A dramatic recreation of past battles is performed for visitors with recorded voices shouting and reacting to orders, "smoke" filling the room and the awesome sound of occasional cannon blasts.

St. Michael's Mount

Continuing almost straight west, we soon came in view of St.

Michael's Mount in Marazion. Ancient Marazion is a bit of an attraction in itself, laying claim to being the oldest town in all of Britain.

But it is St. Michael's that steals the show. This marvelous conglomeration of buildings — part Benedictine monastery, part castle and part palatial residence — traces its roots to before the 15th century. It occupies its own special islet just a couple hundred yards offshore from the heart of Marazion.

Passage to the islet is normally accomplished by hiring one of the small boats in the harbor, but you can make your way on foot for a few brief minutes twice a day when the tide is out.

Stepping ashore at St. Michael's, you immediately notice the magnificent flowers and landscaping. A few minutes of huffing and puffing up a winding stone pathway soon gets you to the west door of the castle. Once inside, a self-guided tour slowly yields the castle's secrets. Every window offers breathtaking views of the grounds, the sea or the nearby coast.

Time passes all too quickly in this romantic outpost.

Penzance

Ten minutes west of St. Michael's lies Penzance, known to theater lovers everywhere as the seaside setting for "The Pirates of Penzance." With a lovely promenade for evening strolls and a seemingly endless supply of quaint shops on meandering streets plus a huge public swimming pool, it lives up to its reputation. It is an ideal base from which to see the far western end of Cornwall.

The accommodations in Penzance are almost limitless, with many options in every price category. We stumbled onto a lovely street above the promenade called Regent Terrace and, once there, had our choice of five small hotels set side by side. We opted for the **Lombard House**.

It had just opened for the season under new management and had a fresh coat of paint on everything. We counted five different wallpapers in our large room and bath, all in rose colors but each with its own distinctive floral pattern.

At $56 per night including breakfast, it was quite reasonable. Tom and Rita Kruge, the gracious owners, threw in lots of local color and sightseeing tips at no extra charge.

Dining alternatives also abound. One of our best finds was the *Seafarers Restaurant* within easy walking distance of the Lombard House. Kevin and Jennifer Knott take genuine pride in their establishment, and it shows in everything, including the spotless china, the hand-picked German wines and the incredibly fresh seafood (dinner for two with wine, $51).

For a wallet-pleasing change of pace, try the busy but intimate *Turks Head Pub*, also an easy walk. The evening special with house wine totaled less than $30.

Land's End

At Land's End, England trickles off into a handful of barren rocks protruding from a restless sea and then nothing. Forewarned that the approach to Land's End was a tourist trap, we drove to St. Just and then on to Cape Cornwall to get the same view from five miles north.

In fact, some of the natives still argue that this cape extends a few feet further west than Land's End. Whatever the truth, you have a spectacular view of both landfalls from the towering cliffs of Cape Cornwall. And you get the added benefit of wandering around for a few minutes in the little farm town of St. Just.

Art-mecca St. Ives

St. Ives is the cultural heart of Cornwall. We picked a misty morning for the short drive over the moors from Penzance to St. Ives, arriving just as the sun was burning through the mist. (Leave your car on the outskirts of St. Ives and walk into town or you will waste valuable time searching for nonexistent parking spots. Besides, the cobblestoned streets of this fascinating village are made for walking.)

The number-one attraction is the Tate Gallery St. Ives, an extension of London's famous Tate Gallery and the home of the St. Ives School of Artists. Modern art is the order of the day and it is hard to pick a favorite from the incredible assemblage of pottery, sculpture and works on canvas.

Also worth a visit is the nearby Barbara Hepworth Museum and Sculpture Garden, founded at the time of her death. Her tiny house is charming, her studio looks like she just stepped out for tea, and the attractive gardens feature many of her best works.

Still fascinated by the area's artistic heritage? Then stop in at several of the art galleries sprinkled throughout the higgledy-piggledy assortment of cottages and courtyards that make up this fishing-village-turned-art-mecca.

Wandering and wondering

Returning to Penzance on a winding back road (the British refer to it as a road that "wiggles"), we discovered our favorite place in all of Cornwall: the ruins of a 2,000-year-old Celtic village called Chysauster. It is located 2½ miles northwest of Gulval on Route B3311.

You park in a small lot next to a stone cottage, then walk several hundred yards on a footpath next to a hedgerow to reach the site. The scenery is breathtaking: a flower-filled meadow overlooking the distant Cornish coast.

Near at hand are the remains of eight stone farmhouses, nestled close together for protection. Each structure was built in the round with an assortment of connected rooms around the perimeter. The inner courtyard was reserved for livestock, chickens and children.

Chysauster is ideal for wandering and wondering. Add a stiff wind and a light mist for atmosphere and you have one of the most enchanting sites imaginable.

While in the area, don't miss Cripplesease Pottery. It is also on Route B3311, roughly halfway between Halsetown and Nancledra. Local artists Jamie and Dodie Herschel turn out some of the most exquisite pottery we found in all of Cornwall. You can watch them work, and the fruits of their labor are for sale at reasonable prices.

King Arthur's place?

Heading back toward London from Penzance, we had time for one more castle. Our choice was

Tintagel on the windswept northwest coast. Legend has long associated Tintagel with King Arthur, Merlin and the Knights of the Round Table.

However, this connection has pretty much been disproved by recent excavations. The current castle dates from the 13th century, long after King Arthur's heyday, although some of the ruins are much, much older.

Whether Tintagel was the home of Christian Celtic monks or the stronghold of Cornish kings from the Dark Ages may never be known. But this does not lessen the site's romantic appeal. The approach is almost mystical as you walk down a path from the village to the sea.

Reaching the bottom, you hear pounding surf and see magnificent caves carved into the rock. The castle itself is on a small island which you reach by climbing a rocky trail and then transversing a narrow bridge suspended high above the swirling water. The views from within are well worth the effort inherent in getting there.

Looking back at Marazion from the heights of St. Michael's Mount.

We savored the environs of Tintagel for several hours, so it was too late to make it back to London that day. Our solution was to opt for a small taste of Devon.

We worked our way through a series of one-lane roads to the tiny village of Dunsford near Exeter in the Teign River Valley. The **Royal Oak Inn** caught our attention, and we soon were the guests of pub owners Guy and Alison Arnold.

On the edge of Dartmoor National Park, Dunsford offers wonderful hiking in a pastoral setting. The village itself is filled with thatched-roof cottages, friendly townsfolk and curious sheep. After a pub dinner at the Royal Oak featuring meat pies with puff crusts rising eight inches high, we were ready for a great night's sleep and a leisurely return to London.

When to go

Cornwall is a March-through-October destination. It gets crowded with British vacationers in the summer and prices skyrocket, so spring and fall are the best time to visit. All you need is a good map of Great Britain, readily available at English gas stations and bookstores, and a mild sense of adventure.

Where to stay

Every town of any size has a local tourist information office with up-to-date information on accommodations. Here are our favorites (prices are in U.S. dollars and are for two persons — off-season — in an en suite room with a full English breakfast):

The Globe Inn, North Street, Lostwithiel; phone 01208 872501 — $60.

Chelsea House Hotel, 2 Emslie Road, Falmouth; phone 01326 212230 — $53.

Lombard House, Regent Terrace, Penzance; phone 01736 64897 — $56.

The Royal Oak Inn, Dunsford in Devon; phone 01647 52256 — $64.

Special notes — Off-season hotel rates are often negotiable, so it pays to bargain. To call any of the above numbers from the U.S., dial 011 for an international line and 44 for the U.K., then drop the zero and dial the rest of the number.

Leeds, the enthusiast's castle

KEITH GEBERS, Elk Grove, CA

Castles have a timeless fascination. In days of long ago, castles meant security, not only for the people who lived there but for the region surrounding the imposing structure. As time progressed and the original reasons for a castle's existence diminished, it still was the symbol of affluence and opulence.

As children we studied castles in school, with the girls being impressed by the grandeur and the boys intrigued by the defense and military interest the structures provided.

Today, England and most of Europe still have the remains of many castles. Fortunately, a lot of them have been restored and have become national treasures.

Striking example

One of the world's most attractive castles is Leeds in Kent. Leeds looks like a castle should. It has majesty without being ostentatious. The grounds are beautifully kept and the castle has an inviting aura.

A light rain was falling as we got our first glimpse of Leeds Castle, and the sight was breathtaking. We had flown to London by British Airways in May '94 to cover some military article possibilities, but a lifelong intrigue with castles was not to be denied.

Called the "Maidstone in Kent," Leeds wears the mantle of being "The loveliest castle in the world." Looking at it, with all its beauty, you know there is a certain livability there not found in most other castles. Leeds appears as sort of a "fantasy" castle, something to inspire a hobbyist to build a model of it.

Yet it is a very real castle, dating back to the days when it was a Norman stronghold. Originally, Leeds was a wooden structure, and it has a history far older than some of the famous castles of Europe that were built during the Renaissance or later.

When you walk down the halls of Leeds, you are following in the footsteps of Edward I, Edward III, Richard II and Henry V. While Henry VIII did not actually live at Leeds, he frequently visited there and spent a fortune to make it virtually a showcase among the world's castles.

As the world's demands and technology changed as the years passed, Leeds fell into disrepair. By the early 1900s it was hardly more than a hulk of falling bricks. In the mid 1920s, newspaper publisher William Randolph Hearst showed an interest in purchasing the castle but was advised against it because it contained few niceties like running water, nor did it have much potential for modern heating installation.

Leeds of that time led to the tale that castles were not really the ornate dwellings we thought but instead were dingy, dank and cold.

Leeds today

Fortunately, the Hon. Olive Paget, who was to become Lady Baillie, purchased the decaying structure and lands and started an extensive restoration project that was to last for years.

Today, the castle retains all of its authentic regality of the past but is comfortable and warm and inviting to visitors. The grounds with their croquet-game settings are delightful. There also are a nice gift shop and restaurant for those who want to embellish their visit to Leeds.

But Leeds is a true castle in every respect. As children, few people realize the difference between a castle and a palace. A palace is merely a residence, but a castle is a virtual fortress, with a moat, parapets and in most cases an armory.

Leeds Castle is no mere tourist attraction, not even today. Its history did not end hundreds of years ago. During WWII, part of the structure was used as a military hospital. Today it remains an important meeting place for heads of state. President Carter hosted the original Middle East Peace Accord meetings at Leeds in the 1970s.

In addition to official functions, Leeds also serves as an excellent festival center. The Festival of English Wines, the Balloon and Vintage Car Fiesta and open-air concerts are just part of the activities at Leeds today.

If you're a castle enthusiast, visit Leeds.

From Land's End to Canterbury

MARGARET PETELA, Berkeley, CA

From a 3-week trip along the south coast of England, traveling from Land's End to Canterbury, I offer the following observations as well as recommendations for accommodations, restaurants, sights and activities.

Practical pointers

Lunch and dinners, even in pubs, were expensive: £4 to £5 (£1 = about US$1.60 in September '95) for just fish and chips, along with the ubiquitous peas. In general, we spent between £7 and £14 per person for dinners, whether seafood, meat or pasta, although it was possible to spend much more.

American-style fresh green salads seemed to be unavailable in Cornwall; fresh vegetables anywhere were few and far between.

Some restaurants were outstanding, however, and are mentioned below. Pizzerias, creperies and Indian and Italian restaurants make a pleasant change when British food begins to pall, as it inevitably does.

At the end of August/early September, the tourist spots in the West Country are very crowded, with long waits at restaurants; make reservations whenever possible. Many British families vacation this time of year, often with three or four very young children.

Despite the summer's drought, weather in September was the usual: some sun, some wind, some light rain, a gale, and never really cold.

Cottage rental

Four adults rented a 3-bedroom farm cottage in St. Endellion, near Port Isaac on the Cornish Atlantic coast, for a week from Castles, Cottages and Flats, Ltd., 7 Faneuil Hall Marketplace, Boston, MA 02109; phone 617/742-6030. The cost was about $675.

From the farmhouse it was possible either to drive or to walk on public footpaths through cow pastures to the hilly, picturesque fishing village of Port Isaac.

There, the **Shipwright Inn** was good for seafood dinner (about £12 apiece, with sassy and pleasant service from the chef's wife), and at the **Slipway Hotel/Restaurant** the bouillabaise was outstanding.

We spent one day riding the flat, easy, car-free biking trail along the beautiful Camel River Estuary between Wadebridge and Padstow, renting bikes from Bridge Bike Hire in Wadebridge (£6 per day. Reserve a day ahead; phone 01208 813050).

In Padstow we sampled wild salmon in sorrell sauce for lunch at Rick Stein's *The Seafood Restaurant*, a world-class establishment serving true gourmet meals. A 3-course prix-fixe lunch was £21.50 and well worth it.

Legend and literature come alive

We enjoyed pottering about nearby Boscastle, a village with an unusual, photogenic harbor and Atlantic-abraded cliffs, and clambering the ruins of Tintagel, a crumbling castle set high above the scouring sea and said by some to be King Arthur's birthplace.

We drove one day on Bodmin Moor, visiting **Jamaica Inn** (gloriously, tackily touristy, with a surprisingly interesting display of Daphne du Maurier's writings and life).

We also visited Dozmary Pool (more a marshy cow pond, containing King Arthur's Excalibur, according to legend), and the Hurlers, a prehistoric stone circle surrounded by moor ponies grazing among abandoned stone-mine engines.

St. Ives and east

Farther south, in St. Ives (a charming, bustling fishing and artists' town), we enjoyed **Derwent Guest House**, 6 Sea View Terrace; phone 01736 797505 (£16 per person per night, breakfast included).

Ask for the family room with a view of the harbor, where seals cavort when the tide is high and colorful fishing boats are stranded when it recedes.

On a day's drive around Land's End peninsula, we visited Chysauster, a mysterious, ruined ancient stone village, and Land's End itself. Penzance and St. Michael's Mount also are nearby.

Heading east, we stayed a few days in Lyme Regis. A spectacular gale there smashed 15-foot breakers against the seawall and hurled fist-sized rocks up onto the marine parade while we were there.

Fossil hunting on Monmouth Beach just west of the Cobb is free and, particularly after a storm, guaranteed to yield a 30-million-year-old ammonite or two for your collection. You can buy a beach guide from The Fossil Shop.

Chichester, Bosham and beyond

Traveling east, we spent an afternoon in Portsmouth visiting Admiral Nelson's historic warship HMS *Victory* and the resurrected Tudor warship *Mary Rose*, both well worth the effort.

Looking for a place to spend the night in the area of Chichester, we discovered the weekend boater's hideaway of Bosham, an ancient village, where King Canute's daughter is reputedly buried in the local church and where the high tide floods the main road twice a day (be careful where you park your car!).

We highly recommend **Barford B&B** in Bosham, run by the charming and accommodating Mary and Tony Flanagan (phone 0243 573393); the price was £18 per person with breakfast.

Worth visiting near Bosham is Fishbourne Roman Palace, with its beautiful intact mosaic floors, and Petworth House, a stately home with a painting collection to rival some big-city museums, including a few by William Blake and several by JMW Turner.

Also nearby is Tangemere Airfield, a WWII airfield and now a museum loaded with interesting memorabilia and some reconstructed aircraft — a good place to spend a rainy afternoon.

On Sunday, the only day we ventured in, all of Chichester, the nearest big town to Bosham, appeared closed.

Battle and Canterbury

As our vacation time drew to a close, we raced east, stopping for an afternoon at Battle, evocative site of the historic Battle of Hastings in 1066, on our way to Canterbury.

In Canterbury, we can highly recommend the **Cathedral Gate Hotel** (phone 0227 464381) on Burgate, literally next door to the main entry gate to Canterbury Cathedral.

For such convenience, with breakfast delivered to the room, we paid £54 per night, although some doubles can be reserved for £45.

Beware the hotel's free car park, however. This weedy lot several blocks away at the end of a deserted alley is just secluded enough to make thievery easy.

When we found our car there with the front passenger window smashed, British AA was on the spot within an hour and in about another hour they had us fitted with a new window and on the road again — all as painlessly as possible under the circumstances.

For lunch or dinner in Canterbury, we highly recommend *Beau's Creperie*, 59 Palace St., serving a variety of filling, delicious dinner and dessert crepes for about £14-£20 for two.

Of course, visiting the mighty cathedral is the main activity here, but shopping Canterbury's busy pedestrian district also is rewarding.

Even after four or five visits, I still find it easy to occupy three weeks in England! Bon voyage.

Waiting for a tour of the HMS Victory.

Portsmouth's ships and naval museum

RITA BERMAN©, Chapel Hill, NC

Anyone interested in ships, maritime history and treasures brought up from the sea, will find a day out at Portsmouth's historic dockyard not long enough to see everything on display, but it will be enough time to give an overview of Britain's naval heritage. An All-in-One entry ticket costs £9.50 (about $15.50) for seniors.

Walk the decks of HMS *Victory*, Nelson's flagship at the Battle of Trafalgar, and HMS *Warrior* (1860), the pride of Queen Victoria's fleet, and you will gain insight into a sailor's life in the last century.

The *Mary Rose*

Going back even further to Tudor times, there is the hull of the *Mary Rose*, Henry VIII's warship that sank before his eyes and plunged almost 700 men, weapons and possessions to the bottom of the Solent in 1545.

Over 400 years later, in 1982, the hull was raised clear of the seabed and transferred underwater into a cradle that was brought to the surface.

When I first visited the *Mary Rose* in June of 1984, I walked across a footbridge in the dry dock temporary ship hall and through the mist looked down on the structure as it was sprayed with chilled water to prevent deterioration.

Revisiting the *Mary Rose* in October 1997, I was astonished at the way the exhibit had been built up with new enclosed viewing galleries that included taped recordings for the education of the viewer.

The hull is a living laboratory as scientists use the latest techniques to preserve the structure. Since 1994 it has been sprayed with a water-soluble wax, polyethylene glycol, which penetrates the wood.

It is estimated the process to preserve the *Mary Rose* will take at least 15 years.

A film about the raising of the ship may be viewed in the Mary Rose Exhibition Hall along with possessions of the sailors and other items from Tudor times.

HMS *Victory*

Nelson's HMS *Victory* is probably the main attraction for most people. This magnificent sailing ship has lured me back several times. It is associated with romance and danger. Its commander was a popular admiral who flouted convention by having a love affair with Lady Hamilton, of which a movie was made.

Nelson led the fleet to victory at the Battle of Trafalgar but was hit by a musket ball and died aboard ship. Every time I tour it I marvel at the cramped quarters in which the men lived, where they cooked, ate, slept and fought.

Timed tours are scheduled in order to accommodate visitors.

HMS *Warrior*

Because of the *Victory* tour schedule it is best to leave viewing HMS *Warrior* to the last, even though it is the first ship you see as you come through the Victory Gate.

This iron-hulled armored battleship was the pride of Queen Victoria's fleet. It was restored and brought to Portsmouth in 1987. It is huge compared to the *Victory* and had a crew of 700 officers and men. There are four decks, which visitors may explore at their leisure with the aid of a deck plan.

Royal Naval Museum

Six galleries in the Royal Naval Museum present 800 years of naval history, from sailing ships through steam and World War II to the Navy today. Figureheads, paintings, uniforms, medals, me-

Ornate wood carving decorates the Victory.

mentos and photographs make up some interesting displays.

After a few hours, you may be looking around for a place to eat. In the exhibition area you will find the *Tradewinds Restaurant*, serving hot meals and snacks, or the *Ship's Biscuit Cafe* for lighter meals.

Getting there

To reach Portsmouth, you can take a train from London; travel time is approximately 1½ hours. The railway station is a few minutes' walk from the exhibition. By car, take the M27 or A27 leading to M275 and follow the Historic Ships' signposts.

In addition to the land exhibits you can take a Portsmouth Harbor cruise or take the ferry to Gosport and climb aboard HMS *Alliance* for a tour of a submarine.

Lavenham, one of England's finest medieval towns

LLOYD McCUNE, Contributing Editor

The Little Star
Twinkle, twinkle, little star;
How I wonder what you are!
Up above the world so high,
Like a diamond in the sky.
As your bright and tiny spark
Lights the traveler in the dark,
Though I know not what you are,
Twinkle, twinkle, little star.
– Jane Taylor (1786)

The first and last stanzas of Jane Taylor's childlike poem aptly set the scene for a visit to what is considered one of England's most charming medieval towns.

It was here that "Twinkle, twinkle, little star" was written in 1786, over 200 years ago at a time when electricity, as we use it today, was unknown.

The house where Isaac Taylor, a famous engraver, dwelt with his wife and two daughters, Jane and Ann, is still standing and it was here that Jane gained a bit of immortality for herself and Lavenham, since her "Twinkle, twinkle, little star" was composed here.

There are over 300 buildings in Lavenham of historic and architectural interest, not the least of which is the Guildhall of Corpus Christi, which dates from the early 1500s (Henry VII was on the throne, 1485-1609) and is an excellent example of a close-studded timber-framed building.

Originally the meeting hall of the Guild of Corpus Christi, it has also served as the town hall, a prison, a workhouse, an alms house and a wool store.

Today it dominates the marketplace and is a National Trust building housing various items of local interest and giving an insight into the past history of this town, especially concerning the cloth industry and how woolen cloth was produced over the centuries with the help of an original loom.

It's open seven months of the year, from late March until the end of October. The tearoom is open for morning coffee, light lunches and afternoon teas. Phone (01787) 247 646.

Lavenham is 35 miles east of Cambridge, 65 miles northeast of London (on the M11) and 25 miles from Harwich.

Sudbury, the home of Thomas Gainsborough (and with a collection of his paintings), is a few miles away, as are a number of other interesting and attractive villages.

For the energetic there is also the Lavenham Walk, which starts at the old railway bridge at the north end of town.

Of special interest is the large, cathedral-like church of St. Peter and St. Paul – a fine example of an East Anglian Cloth church.

Also see the Priory, a timber-framed house formerly inhabited by monks, cloth merchants and Elizabethan rectors (Elizabeth I, 1558-1603). Note the paintings, drawings and stained-glass windows; there also is a unique herb garden. It is closed to visitors at present.

Lodgings in the area include the following:

• **The Swan Hotel**, a Forte, heritage hotel dating from the 14th century (Edward III, 1327-1377; Richard II, 1377-1399) — antique architecture. Rates are £75 single (near US$120) and £140 ($224) double. Phone (01787) 247 477.

• **The Angel Hotel**, first licensed in 1420 — amenities with pleasant garden.

Rates, per room per night, are £37.50-£47.50, £60-£70 and £70-£80 ($60-$75, $95-$111 and $111-$127, respectively). Phone (01787) 247 388.

• **The Great House Hotel & Restaurant** — meals served in both courtyard and dining room.

Rates, per night, including full English breakfast, are £50 ($80) single on weekdays, £75 ($119) single on weekends, £68 ($108) double occupancy on weekdays and £78 ($124) double on Saturdays. Phone (01787) 247 431.

• **The Red House**, a Victorian house with en suite bedrooms. Price per room per night is £45 ($72). Phone (01787) 248 074.

The American connection — there is a strong link between the East Coast of the United States and the East Anglia region, a link dating back to the 17th century.

In April 1630, John Winthrop, from the village of Groton in South Suffolk, set sail for America with 15 ships and 1,000 emigrants. He took with him a charter from Charles I granting wide powers of self- government, with Winthrop himself becoming the first governor of the State of Massachusetts.

East Anglian visitors traveling to Massachusetts today will come across familiar place names such as Sudbury, Acton, Haverhill and Chelmsford, and there are many phrases thought to be "Americanisms" that are, in fact, survivals of the East Anglian dialect spoken by early colonists.

The American Air Force used East Anglia as a base in World War II and some of the airfields are still intact. 1992 was the 50th anniversary of the U.S. servicemen's arrival in this area.

This information is included in a mini-guide to the South Suffolk district. I would like to add the short poem found in the same volume with Jane's famous poem. It is by Charles Wesley (1707-1788), co-founder of the Methodist Church:

Gentle Jesus, meek and mild,
Look upon this little child;
Pity my simplicity,
Suffer me to come to Thee.
Fain I would to Thee be brought,
Gracious God, forbid it not;
In the Kingdom of Thy grace,
Grant this little child a place.

(In memory of Frieda M. Young of Lavenham who helped prepare the text.)

A Hampshire village

RITA BERMAN©, Chapel Hill, NC

The little village of Chawton in East Hampshire, England, draws many Jane Austen fans. Jane Austen lived there the last eight years of her life, from 1809 until 1817. It was there that she revised the novels she had commenced in her early twenties.

You can take a train from London to the market town of Alton, but you need a car to get to Chawton village. Signs for Chawton and Jane Austen's 17th-century house, now turned into a museum, are at the roundabout off the junction of A31 with A32, which is one mile southwest of Alton.

This is an accessible museum—no roped-off areas. It's furnished with period furniture, books, prints and Austen mementos, including a lock of her hair and a quilt which she and her mother and sister made. There is some dispute as to whether the writing table is actually the one she used.

The museum is open daily April to October and on selected days of the week in the winter months.

Soaking up atmosphere

Away from the hurly-burly of London, I found it restful to stroll in the atmosphere of this little byway with its cottages and *The Greyfriar* pub and restaurant opposite the Austen museum on Winchester Road.

I paid $33 for a 3-course homemade lunch for two; the main entree was poached salmon with heaps of vegetables.

Exiting from The Greyfriar, you'll notice that the road forks. The right fork takes you back to the A31 junction. The left fork leads to the old parish church where members of the Austen family are buried, but not Jane. She died in Winchester on July 18, 1817, and is buried in Winchester Cathedral.

Next door to the parish church is Chawton House, a rambling, rundown, 51-room house that formerly was the summer residence of the Knight family. Jane's brother Edward was adopted by the Knight family and he inherited this property.

Jane Austen is said to have strolled there. My cousin and I did the same. A small deer ran out right in front of us, then a rabbit. The sun shown and birds sang overhead. Delightful.

Close to Chawton is Selborne, which offers the historic house and garden of Gilbert White, the I8th-century naturalist. White and his brother constructed the Zig Zag Path (now under the care of the National Trust) that leads to the top of a steep hanger with magnificent views across the countryside.

More information on East Hampshire is available from The Tourist Information Center, 7 Cross and Pillory Lane, Alton, Hampshire, England GU34 1HL.

Burford House Hotel — the Cotswolds, England.

Burford in the Cotswolds

JUNE GRIFFIN, Lewiston, ME

On my many visits to England in the past, I have seen the Cotswolds area; I've even stayed at Cheltenham and Broadway. On this trip, however, in late October '96, traveling with my son Richard from Boston — his first time to the U.K. — we stayed in the delightful small town of Burford.

An ancient market town that flourished at the height of the wool trade, Burford is so old that it was mentioned in the Domesday Book in 1086. It became prosperous in the Middle Ages, its importance seen today in the many imposing buildings still there, including the magnificent Church of St. John the Baptist which dates back to Norman times.

Burford remains unchanged in appearance, even though the wool trade has vanished, and the main street is lined with lovely old houses made of soft, golden Cotswold limestone, most with slate roofs, flowers in window-boxes and small gardens.

This street, High Street, runs down the hill to the Windrush River, which offers a lovely 2-mile country walk along its banks.

From Oxford to Burford

Burford calls itself "The Gateway to the Cotswolds," as it is 20 miles northwest of Oxford, where we arrived by train on a Sunday morning. We had reservations at the **Burford House Hotel**, right in town on High Street.

I discovered that much closes down Sunday morning, so I had arranged with the hotel owners, Simon and Jane Henty, for a car and driver to pick us up at the Oxford train station for the half-hour ride to Burford.

Valerie Keylock was the guide and driver and knew the area well, as she lived there. She charged 20 pounds (about US$32 at £1= US$1.60) for the ride and suggested that for an extra $25 she would drive us for an hour with stops at some well-known Cotswold villages like Bourton-on-the-Water, Upper and Lower Slaughter and Stow-on-the-Wold.

Driving out of Oxford, we saw the spires of the famous university and a few miles outside the city had a view, from the gateway, of Blenheim Palace, the Marlborough family home, birthplace of Winston Churchill.

Renting your own car is the best way to see the Cotswolds, but there was plenty to see and do in Burford on foot. Shops are open on Sunday and there were antique shows at several locations.

Historic lodgings

Burford House Hotel is small and charming — just seven rooms, all doubles, some with 4-poster beds and huge bathrooms. Including full English breakfast, rates for two people ranged from 65 pounds ($104) up to 95 pounds ($152), high season being from May to October.

The building is very old, the middle section dating from the 1500s. The front was restored 150 years ago using old materials to make the distinctive black-and-white-striped front, the lower half of the yellow Cotswold stone building.

The hotel serves breakfast, lunch and a wonderful afternoon tea. High tea costs 7.75 pounds ($12.40) and is served before a fireplace, with scones, jam and clotted cream and fruitcake and tarts. A private room is kept for house guests and a larger room is open to the public for lunch and tea.

Cotswolds highlights

Located in southern England, the Cotswolds — an area roughly

June Griffin at statue shop on High Street, Burford.

between Bath in the south and Stratford-upon-Avon in the north — consists of a range of limestone hills and rich pastureland with flocks of sheep, famous for their wool.

Food is excellent in these country towns, from pastry and tea shops to restaurants like the *Angel Inn & Restaurant* on Witney Street in Burford, where we had a fine Sunday dinner of roast beef; two courses with coffee cost 10.95 pounds ($17.50).

With a BritRail Pass for southeast England ($119 a person), travel was easy and could be done at our own time and choice. Burford was a high spot on this trip.

Booking tips

For hotel booking information, contact Simon and Jane Henty, Burford House Hotel, 99 High Street, Burford, Oxfordshire, England X18 4QA; phone 01993 823151, or fax 01993 823240.

In Burford, you can phone our driver/guide, Valerie Keylock, at 01993 823234.

Cloister of Furness Abbey.

An archaeological ramble through England's Lake District

JULIE SKURDENIS, Contributing Editor

In England's Lake District, mountains are called fells, streams are becks or rills and lakes are tarns.

In places, its beauty is untamed and savage and in others, peaceful and gentle. It's the reason I keep returning to the Lake District, undeniably one of England's most famed scenic areas.

But it isn't just nature that draws me there. Located 300 miles northwest of London, this scenically rich area also is archaeologically blessed. Dozens of sites pepper the area, representing four-and-a-half thousand years (and more) of human occupation.

Castlerigg

Among the oldest sites is Castlerigg, located near the town of Keswick in the north of the Lake District.

Castlerigg is a stone circle with its origins in the Neolithic period, roughly 2500 B.C. It is similar to the many henges found throughout Britain (Stonehenge being among the best known).

Many henges have banks and ditches enclosing a circle of stones. Castlerigg lacks both bank and ditch but does have an unusual rectangular arrangement of stones, dubbed the "sanctuary," set within the stone circle on its eastern side. What its function once was we don't know.

The stone circle itself, composed of almost 60 stones, none higher than seven feet, probably was used as a central meeting place by the scattered local tribes of this area. They may have gathered there to buy, sell and exchange.

The circle also might have been used for religious functions or perhaps as a "calendar" for calculating the seasons.

It might possibly have served all of these functions at different times in its existence.

Castlerigg's location atop a knoll ensures it a breathtaking panoramic view of the surrounding fells, even with the mist often softening and sometimes obscuring the outlines of the surrounding hills.

A long leap of two-and-a-half thousand years leads to the period of the Roman occupation of Britain. The Romans arrived on the island in A.D. 43 and by the '70s had reached the Lake District.

To subjugate the Brigantes, a troublesome local tribe, they built a series of forts crisscrossing enemy territory. One of these forts, Galava, was located at present-day Ambleside beside Lake Windermere in the center of the Lake District.

The earliest turf and timber fort was replaced during the reigns of Emperors Trajan and Hadrian (A.D. 98-138).

Rectangular in shape, this new stone fort enclosed a commander's house, a headquarters and granaries as well as barracks capable of housing 500 soldiers. A stone wall with four corner turrets and four gateways surrounded the whole.

Today's visitor can cross a park beside the lake to visit what's left of the fort. Tall grass covers the site, but it's not difficult to trace the outlines of the various buildings that once existed there. Cows graze alongside.

Dacre

The tiny village of Dacre outside the market town of Penrith in the northeast corner of the Lake District is steeped in history, much of it concentrated around its church and castle.

The Venerable Bede in his "Ecclesiastical History," written in A.D. 731, mentions an Anglo-Saxon monastery at Dacore (Dacre). Excavations have revealed a cemetery predating the Conquest of 1066.

Although no one is exactly sure

when the present stone church was built, the earliest known rector is Nicolas de Appleby, who lived in the 13th century.

Inside Dacre Church are two ancient cross shafts. The older is ninth-century Anglian with intricate carvings of humans, beasts, flowers and vines. There's an intriguing winged lion sporting a moustache.

Beside the Anglian cross remnant is a Viking fragment carved between 900 and 1000. Among the four carved panels is one of Adam and Eve with Eve reaching up to pick an apple. Unlike most representations depicting Eve as naked before the Fall, this Eve wears a skirt.

Four stone bears mark the corners of Dacre's graveyard. Carved sometime in the Middle Ages — no one is sure when — the bears relate a mini-drama in stone: bear sleeping, bear looking at cat that has jumped onto its back, bear trying to swipe cat and bear looking smug after devouring cat.

Dacre Castle stands only a few hundred feet beyond the Dacre graveyard. It's one of the dozens of fortified towers, called *pele* towers, erected in the 13th and 14th centuries to protect the area against marauding Scots from farther north.

Furness Abbey

Far south in the Lake District is Furness Abbey, at one time the second-richest Cistercian monastery in England (Fountains Abbey in Yorkshire was the richest). For almost 400 years, Furness thrived from its establishment in 1147 until its dissolution in 1537 during the reign of Henry VIII.

Julie in the chapter house of Furness Abbey.

Today those centuries of prosperity are abundantly evident as one walks about the manicured ruins, which contain the church where medieval monks worshipped, the cloister where they studied and perambulated, the

200-foot-long dormitory where they slept and the infirmary where they recuperated when ill.

The remains of the chapter house where the monks gathered to discuss abbey business is especially beautiful with twin lancet windows. Book cupboards for storing manuscripts lie on either side of the entrance to the chapter house.

The day we visited, Furness Abbey was thronged with schoolchildren, sketchbooks in hand. They imparted life to the long-deserted buildings. One sat conscientiously sketching the *reredorter*, or latrine, that once stood over a stream a few feet behind the monks' dormitory.

Just outside Penrith stand the haunting remnants of Brougham Castle on a grassy mound beside the River Eamont.

The earliest portion of the medieval castle — the keep — was built by Robert de Vipont early in the 13th century.

Over the next 450 years, various Viponts and Cliffords (they married into the Vipont family) added on.

The keep can be climbed for a panoramic view over castle and countryside. One can look out over the ruins of the great chamber, hall, kitchen and chapel toward the sturdy tower meant as additional defense for the castle.

Beside the castle lie the unexcavated remains of Brocavum, a Roman fort built strategically at the point where the roads to Scotland and the city of York intersect. Brocavum was linked to the network of forts crisscrossing the Lake District including Galava at Ambleside.

Even our "home away from home" on this trip fit in with our archaeological orientation. We rented a 17th-century farmhouse in the tiny village of Helton not far from Ullswater, one of the most lovely of the Lake District's many lakes.

Built in 1667 — during the reign of the Stuart king Charles II — "our" house, Town End, had its own large garden, two sitting rooms each with fireplace, four bedrooms (one with a four-poster), two bathrooms and a resident ghost.

The best time of day was late afternoon after a day of archaeological exploration when we'd make ourselves a cup of tea, take it out to the garden, watch the shadows lengthen across the patchwork of fields lying in front of the house and pretend we were lords of the manor.

The cost? $1,050 for a week in high season or about $150 per night (for an entire house). No charge for the ghost.

Contact British Travel Associates, P.O. Box 299, Elkton, VA 22827; 800/ 327-6097.

If you go. . .

We flew Virgin Atlantic from New York to London. Even in economy class, there was a multichoice video selection system making it possible to squeeze in three movies on the flight across the Atlantic.

We then drove the 300 miles, most of it on motorway, to the Lake District. The village of Helton is just off the M6 motorway.

The Plough Inn, built in the 1700s, was originally part of the Wigglesworth Estate. It later became an alehouse and today has a restaurant, bar and guest rooms.

Still wondering about Wigglesworth

ROCHELLE OLDFIELD, Walnut Creek, CA

You may remember the movie "Zorro the Gay Blade" starring George Hamilton. You probably don't remember that Zorro's brother was Bunny Wigglesworth. For some reason, that name always stuck in my mind. Years later I found out that my husband's family came from a village in England called Wigglesworth. Ever since then I was determined to go there.

Just as imagined

In winter British Airways offered a low-priced fare to London. I decided that this was the time to go. I knew it would be cold and stormy, but, then again, that would only make it more cozy.

You won't find Wigglesworth on a map of England. I found it by calling the British Tourist Authority. They told me it was located in the Yorkshire Dales.

I purchased a map of that area and there it was, on one of those tiny lines indicating a secondary road. It was just east of Tosside, south of Giggleswick and next to the River Ribble.

We rented a car at Heathrow

Airport in London. Driving in England was a first for both of us. By some miracle we negotiated our first roundabout without any mishap and found the M6 Motorway going north. We settled into an uneasy drive. The radio was on. A weather report announced that another storm was coming, with snow predicted.

About six hours later we left the M6 at Junction 31. From this point on, the landscape and feeling of the country changed. It was the English countryside that I had always imagined.

It was a land of sheep and small farms. The rolling hills were parceled into individual pastures by old, moss-covered stone walls. The gray farmhouses were lonely and forbidding. In most cases the only sign of life was a wisp of coal smoke from a century-old chimney pot.

There were fat, black-faced sheep grazing everywhere. Some huddled against the stone walls to escape the cold.

We followed a comfortable road for some time before coming upon a sign that pointed us to Wigglesworth. A left turn took us onto a narrow winding road bordered on each side by a hedgerow of bramble.

The only traffic was sheep. We followed a middle-aged gentleman in a wool cap and down jacket and his dog for several miles as he herded his sheep to a new pasture. He finally turned off after crossing a stone bridge.

Wigglesworth's inn

As we followed, the sky turned dark and a light snow started to fall. Soon the green pastures were covered in white. I looked to my left and just made out a historic marker that read "Wigglesworth Hall." Another quarter mile and we reached a crossroads. This was the start of the village of Wigglesworth.

I had read that there was a place to stay there and hoped that I was correct. It was snowing heavily now and neither one of us felt like driving anymore.

The town consists of about five buildings. One of them is the **Plough Inn**. The whitewashed stone building looked deserted, but we parked anyway. As we approached the door I noticed that the windows sported traditional dimpled glass panes. These, I was to learn later, originated in the 1700s.

As we entered we were warmly greeted by Brian Goodall. He told us that the inn had a restaurant, bar and guest rooms. The rooms were 30 pounds per person and breakfast was included in the price.

I looked around and saw a cozy, wood-burning fireplace right next to the old wooden bar. The walls were covered with polished brass artifacts. There was a sitting room decorated with the work of local artists, a wood-paneled dining room with a fireplace and a small library stocked with a variety of books.

Brian led us up a narrow flight of stairs to the second floor and then down a low-ceilinged hallway. The guest room was beautifully decorated in an English country style. I decided that we were definitely going to stay.

Later, Brian told us about the inn. He said that it was built in the 1700s and was originally part of the Wigglesworth Estate. It became an alehouse in 1750. Many of the timbers that cross the ceiling are original. He pointed out the unusual sash windows. He told us that a fire in the 1940s had destroyed part of the building; however, that part has been rebuilt. Our room was located in that area.

It was called the Plough Inn because this was farmland and inns are frequently named after something typical of the area where they are located. Brian said that his family had owned the inn for some time. He ran it by himself in the winter while his parents vacationed in the Caribbean.

Country atmosphere

In the summer the area offers excellent fishing, hiking and bicycling. Three mountain peaks popular with hikers can be seen to the north: Ingleborough, Pen-y-ghent and Whernside.

We told Brian that my husband's ancestors came from Hill Top Farm in Wigglesworth and he gave us directions. The snow had stopped, so we decided to try to find it.

As we left, my husband jokingly asked him if the inn had any ghosts. Brian answered somewhat defensively that he had never seen one.

There are a number of farms in the area and they each have a name. Most date back to the 1400s. The houses are gray-stone structures surrounded by barns and storage buildings.

We found Hill Top Farm with some difficulty. It was up a one-lane road at the top of a hill. We took several pictures. It was snowing heavily again so we decided to return.

The bar and restaurant opened at 7 p.m. We went downstairs at that time for a long-awaited pint of bitter. We were surprised to find that there were other guests. There were two craftsmen, in Wigglesworth to install windows, and a couple vacationing from their home in Blackpool; they ran a resort there and explained that in the summer Blackpool was one of England's popular vacation spots.

At about 7:30 Brian came around and took everyone's order for dinner. We could eat wherever we wanted to. We decided to sit in the dining room next to the fireplace. We had excellent Scottish salmon, a bottle of claret and, for dessert, cheese and biscuits.

It had been a long day, so we retired early. Just before bed I looked out the window and could just make out the red English phone booth across the street. The snow was getting deeper. It looked like we were going to be snowed in. I thought that this was a pretty good place for that to happen.

. . . and things that go bump in the night

I quickly fell into a sleep filled with strange dreams. This frequently happens when I travel. I don't know if I was dreaming at the time, but I recall hearing three clicks as if someone were opening the door to our room. I felt someone pressing their hand into my upper back. I gasped. I looked around. The door was closed, there was no one there. I pulled the blanket over my head and went back to sleep.

The storm had passed and it was bright and sunny the next morning. The snowplows had already cleared the road.

I had the full English grill for breakfast, which consisted of eggs, bacon, sausage, cooked tomato, toast, marmalade and black pudding. Don't ask about that. We paid our bill and said our good-byes.

Stepping out into the bone-chilling cold, I looked at a spectacular view of snow-covered mountains and the upper Ribble Valley. Secretly I thought of coming back in the summer when I could rent a bike and ride down the narrow roads past centuries-old farmhouses.

On the way out of town we stopped at the general store and post office to send a postcard to my husband's father. We wanted it to be postmarked "Wigglesworth."

As we were about to leave, my husband asked the clerk if the inn had any ghosts.

She said, "Oh, yes. There were two women killed there in a fire in 1945. The ghost of one is said to walk the halls trying to warn the other of the impending doom."

She added that the ghost was not malevolent, just helpful.

I thought about the last 24 hours. We had survived a flight to London, a 7-hour drive on the left side of the road, a blizzard and — finally — a ghost. In the process, we found a wonderful English country inn and the home of my husband's ancestors.

I thought, "What else does this trip have in store for us?"

If you go. . .

The Plough Inn is a 3-star inn, which in 1995 was awarded the Les Routiers Casserole Mark of Excellence. The bedrooms are all en suite with breakfast included.

The address is Wigglesworth, Skipton, North Yorkshire BD23 4JR, United Kingdom; phone 01144 (1729) 840243 or fax 01144 (1729) 840243.

To get there, leave the M6 at Junction 31 and take the A59 toward Clitheroe. At Sawley, take the Wigglesworth and Settle road to Wigglesworth (seven miles).

There are several things to see and do in the area. A few miles from Wigglesworth is the town of Settle. This is where England's most scenic railway, the Settle-Carlisle, starts.

There is Skipton Castle, Bolton Abbey for bird-watching and Ingleton Falls. There are eight golf courses within a 30-minute drive. There also are a lot of hiking and bicycling trails.

For more information, call the British Tourist Authority at 800/ 462-2748, or write to Skipton Tourist Office, 9 Sheep St., North Yorkshire BD23 1JH, Unlted Kingdom.

For bike rentals, contact Three Peaks Mountain Bikes, located in Horton-in-Ribblesdale; phone 0729-7860200.

A detailed map of the area can be found in any good travel store in your area. I purchased mine from Estate Publications in England. There was no problem in sending pounds through the mail. Write Bridewell House, Tenterden, Kent, TN30 6EP United Kingdom, or phone 011 441 580-764225.

Luncheon on the lawn at Hartwood House. David and Rosemary Freemantle are to the right.

Private visits to English gardens from a Somerset country home

J. NORVILL JONES, Alexandria, VA

Calling all garden lovers. If you want to spend a week in gardeners' heaven, join David and Rosemary Freemantle on one of their week-long house parties at their lovely country home, Hartwood House, in Somerset County, England.

All-inclusive holiday

My wife, Jackie, and I learned of David and Rosemary's operation through a friend of a friend. Although neither of us is a dedicated gardener, we both enjoy flowers and puttering around our modest suburban spread.

After reading the Freemantle's informative brochure, we and our longtime friends, Bill and Lucille Martin, both avid gardeners, signed on. We found that their brochure does not do justice to the unique experience in store for their guests.

Somerset County lies in the heart of England's finest garden country. Every other week in spring and summer, the Freemantles entertain a maximum of six people as their house guests for a tour of the best gardens illustrating that week's particular theme.

Their brochure states that "your holiday price is complete" and they mean just that. From the time David picks up his guests in London to drive them the 135 miles to Hartwood House until a week later when he delivers them to Heathrow or Gatwick, they need not spend a pence.

All transportation, meals, wine and drinks, guides, entrance fees and even a year's membership in the American arm of the British National Trust are included in one reasonable price.

The price varies with the time of year and the theme for each week. We chose Rose Week. It was a bargain. (1999 price was £1,000, or about $1,600).

Relaxation a sure thing

Hartwood House lies off a country lane between the Quantock Hills to the east, for a time home to Wordsworth and Coleridge, and the Brendon Hills to the West. There the one-lane byways are bordered by ancient hedgerows which, with their frequent junctions, create the appearance of a large-scale maze.

Encountering another vehicle demands courtesy and common sense, attributes often missing on American highways. But this is an unhurried land and the driver giving way merely blinks his lights to signal "I'll do it" and backs up to where there may be a few additional feet to pull over a bit more.

The pace of life in this area was illustrated by a sign outside a small village: "Caution: Free Range Children and Animals."

The Freemantle's comfortable Edwardian house, two miles from the village of Crowcombe, lies in a bucolic setting with extensive flower and vegetable gardens surrounded by woods and farmland. Sheep graze contentedly on land they allow a local farmer to use.

Two friendly black Labs—one old and completely blind and her offspring, Dozer, who is particularly fond of retrieving thrown objects — welcome visitors. They always are on hand to greet the returning van. (Dozer, with anything from a shoe to his food bowl in his mouth, seeks out a guest with a good throwing arm. He always finds a partner.)

Contagious enthusiasm

We were there to see gardens, and gardens of all shapes and sizes, each grand in its own way, we did see. A typical day would begin with a bountiful breakfast including David's favorite item, the leftover dessert, or "pud," as he called it, from the previous night's dinner.

Then it was into the van, usually outfitted with picnic and/or tea supplies, and off to the gardens. We would visit, perhaps, two gardens in the morning, have a picnic or pub lunch, see several more in the afternoon, take a tea break and then return to Hartwood House.

After a bit of rest in our comfortable room, with its large private bath, we gathered in the guests' common room for cocktails and conversation.

Then came the high point of the day: Rosemary's dinner. How she was able to entertain and educate us all day and, in perhaps an hour, produce a multicourse gourmet dinner each night was a mystery to me.

David, a retired British naval officer, ran a "taut ship" and, with good humor and firmness, kept us on the day's course. Rosemary was formerly a teacher of physical education.

Both were not only knowledgeable gardeners but also fonts of in-

Flowers in the East Garden Court at the 16th-century Montacute House.

formation about the local history, geography and people. They made a capable team.

Both hold Royal Horticultural Society qualifications, have exhibited flowers and vegetables in Society shows and have judged in others. Their enthusiasm for gardening is contagious and by week's end I was mentally revamping my own garden domain.

Such gardens, Pimms No. 1 and Squidgy Chocolate Roll

During the course of our stay we visited more than 20 gardens, ranging from the grandeur of National Trust properties such as Mottisfont Abbey and its world-famous rose gardens to private cottage gardens open only one weekend a year.

We saw roses at their best — climbing, hybrid tea, floribunda and old-fashioned — growing up walls, over pergolas, up pillars, in mixed borders and as hedges.

Although rose week was the theme, we saw flowers, plants, trees and landscape settings across the horticultural spectrum. To complement the garden scene, there were fields of yellow rape, blue flax, golden ripe wheat, green barley and oats throughout the countryside.

In the wide range of gardens we visited, my favorites were not those of the historic grand manor houses but the cottage gardens whose owners had, in effect, created silk purses from sows' ears.

At "Reed's Court" in the village of Lydeard St. Lawrence, a retired professional lady had taken a dilapidated 1580 cottage and, wheelbarrow-full by wheelbarrow-full, turned its once barren surroundings into a series of interconnected outdoor rooms of beauty.

And at Pat and Kevin Chittenden's "Vellacott" we were shown around the colorful garden they have created in seven years of retirement. While sipping Pimms No. 1 Cup at sunset, we admired their handiwork of transforming a 16th-century cottage on a hill overlooking Crowcombe into a showplace.

Later they joined us at Hartwood House for our last — and only formal coat-and-tie — dinner. It was a feast of leg of lamb accompanied by carrots, potatoes, squash, flatbeans and turnips from the Freemantle garden plus Rosemary's Squidgy Chocolate Roll—that night's "pud," as the finale.

Steeped in atmosphere

Good company, beautiful gardens, comfortable accommodations and fine food and wine are not the only attractions for guests at Hartwood House. Add to that the beauty of the Somerset area countryside.

One day after wandering through the garden of thatch-roofed Ashtree Cottage, we spread our blankets near a Druidic circle on top of White Sheet Down and picnicked among masses of buttercups while looking down on tidy, hedge-rowed fields of wheat and rape on one side and the remains of a terraced Roman settlement on the other.

Then there was the drive across barren, windblown Exmoor down to picturesque Bossington for a Devon cream tea in the garden of a 16th-century thatch-roofed cottage. On one evening, drinks and dinner at the *Fitzhead Pub* with a lively crowd of locals was a special treat.

Another day, in Crowcombe, Ian Billinge showed us through the village's 15th-century church with its unusual bench-end carvings and a belltower with six bells molded before 1400. Ian and David are both bell-ringers at the church.

A local art show was being held that day at the church house across the lane, a structure reputed to be one of the finest examples of a medieval English church hall.

Day after day, David and Rosemary, with their knowledge, insights and enthusiasm, made their corner of England come alive for us.

One day, as we made our way over the Quantock Hills to Hartwood House after visiting the Longstock Water Gardens, we saw in the distance a bank of clouds rolling in from the Bristol Channel and flowing down the side of the Brendon Hills. When we neared Crowcombe we became enveloped in a thick fog —the cloud had come to Earth.

As David drove carefully down that foggy lane, I felt that I had

A 15th-century cottage in Bossington where you can enjoy Devon cream tea.

become an observer in a landscape out of a Thomas Hardy novel. As an Anglophile, I felt very much at home.

To get in touch

At the end of Rose Week we left Hartwood House most reluctantly. Although we were paying guests, I never felt like a customer; David and Rosemary truly made me feel like a welcome guest in their home.

I highly recommend the remarkable service offered by the Freemantles. They can be reached at Hartwood House, Crowcombe Heathfield, Nr. Taunton, Somerset TA4 4BS, England; phone 011-44-1984-66-7202; fax 011-44-1984-66-7508; e-mail *101537.2334@compuserve.com*.

Their U.S. agent is Ruth Hughes, Holiday Travel, Inc., 2112 W. 25th St., Lawrence, KS 66047; phone 800/346-4387.

Exeter Maritime Museum

MAXINE CIAPPINI, Portland, OR

During one of our forays, my husband and I found the Exeter Maritime Museum at the Haven, Exeter, Devon, England. It's a bit difficult to find the Haven, but the friendly folks of Exeter will help you. We had to ask twice.

This museum celebrates man's ingenuity in using materials at hand to develop waterborne craft. On display are full-sized boats, some no more than rafts, from ancient to modern times and from every continent and culture.

This is not the usual collection of model tall ships in glass cases. Some larger boats are floating in the canal and can be boarded. There are canoes, dhows, a junk, a working steamboat, many racing sailboats and a hand-operated ferry to cross the canal.

There is even a children's play yard that looks like the deck of an old galleon where the kids can climb to the crow's nest, shout orders and haul lines. It's handy if the children get tired of looking at displays before you do. An old-salt volunteer was supervising on the day we were there.

It is an active museum. While we were there we observed a kayaking class for disabled young people on the canal.

It is open all year except Christmas and Boxing Day. Hours are 10 a.m.-5 p.m. in winter and 10-6 p.m. from July through September.

Mud did not keep us indoors, though the paths had occasional places of pure quagmire.

Slow-paced walking tour

MARTY RAUCH, Los Angeles, CA

It was time for a different trip, my travel agent and I agreed. Thus, we explored walking tours — slow paced — which would give me a chance to smell the proverbial roses, strolling through the byways that are bypassed by high-speed trains, tour buses and even rental cars.

I wasn't brave enough to try the walk in Provence because I couldn't imagine flying to Paris and then taking two trains, while struggling in a language and currency I don't know, to get to the village where the walk began.

So off I went to England in May for 10 days of history, ruins, gardens, cottages reminiscent of Alice in Wonderland, sheep meadows and, despite every negative you've heard about British cuisine, elegant food.

There also were more rain, mud and hiking than anticipated, but more coddling, too.

Steve Austin, of Great British Vacations, was guide/host extraordinaire. Knowledgeable about his homeland, its legends and its language, he also is a bon vivant, providing his groups with lavishness at moderate prices.

"Steve likes to live well," whispered a fellow walker one evening, as Steve discussed ordering the wine.

Roughing it?

The public footpaths of England are a marvel — clearly marked, maintained and enjoyed. Be sure to buy ordnance maps to mark your day's high spots.

Our group was small: eight mature ladies and a gentleman friend of Steve's. We were a brief hour out of London but in a world apart. We stayed for five days each at two delightful hotels in two small towns.

A little van took us to our starting point each morning and picked us up at the end of our 6- to 8-mile daily amble. This was not roughing it,

We saw Stonehenge in the rain, which wasn't all bad as it kept down the crowds, so our group moved in for a closer look. We also went to Avebury, another circle of silent stones, a more primitive display with fewer visitors. Again we saw evidence of a place of great significance, even if we can only hypothesize at the meaning.

Old Sarum, with the remains of fortifications and castles, suddenly seemed modern.

Touring gardens

In Bibury we chanced upon a garden tour benefiting the church there, which dates to Saxon days. We visited one sweet-faced woman, surrounded by multihued blossoms perfectly timed to bloom on schedule who admitted her hobby now required the help of a hired hand one day each week.

In an L-shaped plot, a man reading his paper let us admire his work: carefully raised beds were adorned with lots of little plaster garden figures.

Another home featured a beautiful lawn leading down to a gentle bend in the river, only a small cultivated area was near the house.

At Stourhead Gardens we viewed a lavish home and a garden complete with grottoes, sculptures and rare plants. Garden clubs arrange tours to view the splendor. The 2-mile walk around the main garden is wheelchair accessible.

Other visits

At Hailes Abbey, walls and foundation stones indicate the size of a magnificent thanksgiving tribute built by the Earl of Cornwall after his rescue at sea. The dedication, in 1251, attracted King Henry III and Queen Eleanor, every nobleman in the countryside and 13 bishops.

Certainly that group was more fashionable than our disheveled, sometimes muddy, touring party on our return to home base. However, we were welcomed with warmth, if sometimes amusement.

Steve's mother, who lives in Stanton, joined us on our walk, by chance on our rainiest day. Umbrella at the perfect Mary Poppins angle, she told me the lovely story of her daughter's wedding on the great lawn at Castle Combe.

There was a home on this site since before the Norman conquest. Now it boasts a helicopter pad for guests anxious to enjoy what has been voted the prettiest village in England, almost unchanged since the great wool-weaving wealth of the 15th and 16th centuries.

It's pretty enough that Castle Combe provided the background for the film "Dr. Doolittle:" Villagers, including Mrs. Austin, acted as extras.

Accommodations

The single supplement on this walking tour was a whopping $300. My travel agent (Charlotte Coblence of Dunhill Travel in Woodland Hills, CA) was concerned over the frequent tour device of allotting the least-desirable rooms to singles. She was assured that all rooms at the **Rose & Crown** were equally attractive.

My room, in the older section, was a stunner. It had beamed ceilings, antique furniture and a pretty table set up with tea, coffee, cocoa and those butter-laden shortbread biscuits.

The room was large, with a big closet, lovely bathroom and a pink terry robe. (I had always considered those hotel robes an affectation. This robe was as comforting as a kid's teddy bear.)

In the spiffy new part of the Swan, however, the architect did manage to cram every usual amenity into a teeny room. The bathroom boasted an enormous mirror above the basin, with a full-length mirror on each side of the door. But the hair dryer, hard wired into the closet on an 18-inch cord, was not provided with a mirror. Someone flunked Interior Design 101.

Still, I cherish my dearly won privacy and am sensitive about my poor sleeping habits. I tend to read, watch TV, wander or eat at 2:17 or 3:41 a.m. and could not inflict that on a fellow vacationer.

A bit of elegance

Both hotel dining rooms made up for any minor lack; historically and architecturally they were treasures. Rose & Crown's dining room, with French doors on two sides, looked across a curve in the river to a small farm and to the 13th-century Gothic Cathedral of Salisbury, with its spire 27 inches out of plumb.

Dinners offered choices among nine appetizers, 11 entrees and eight desserts. There were old standbys and new items each night for diversity.

We walked past the ancient stones at Avebury, even older and more mysterious than Stonehenge.

Only by crying pitifully, and early, could we have coffee served with dessert rather than in lonely splendor later. Ah, the cultural differences that divide us.

The mezzanine dining room at the Swan, tucked under the cathedral beamed ceiling, lacked the view but served similarly elegant dinners. It had beautiful furniture, china and octagonal gold-

and silver-colored metal place mats to protect the wood tables against hot plates.

Our farewell banquet at the Swan was in a private dining room in the oldest part of the hotel. Candelabra and flowers adorned the table and tapestries softened the stone walls.

Pampered trekking

We ate at pubs in villages along our way—Steve is a pub authority. On the one day that lunchtime did not find us close to a Steve favorite we shopped in a village bake shop for homemade rolls stuffed with ham and cheese and veggies.

The adjoining grocery store provided water, soft drinks and a bit of comparison shopping.

Each morning, breakfast was a splendid array of choices: there was a buffet of juice, cold cereal, yogurt, rolls and fruit; cooked items were offered by a server, and that full English breakfast —eggs, bacon, bangers and blood sausage—was fine for those planning to plow the south 40.

Service went so smoothly, it took a day or so before we realized the Swan's main kitchen was across the road, in the oldest part of the building.

Our servers, in traditional black-and-white uniforms and appearing to be an average age of 14, had to run across the street to fill our oatmeal orders. The only thing that caused them trouble was that we don't call it porridge.

Because my group was made up of experienced travelers (I was the only first-time walker), their worldliness made them especially supportive of my being a loner.

I did lag behind, sometimes, not merely because of my age but my 5-foot-zip height offered an impediment to striding as surely as the 5'10" woman.

As my 5-year-old grandson Alex says, after a special day, "I had an adventure." So did I. And I hope to go again.

Contact Great British Vacations, 800/452-8434.

Author in the Lake District of northwestern England.

From the mountains to the moors — walking alone across England

ROBERT E. BUCKLEY, Marion, IA

In September 1996 I walked across England — a 61st-birthday present from my wife.

Five-star walk

The walk is called the Coast-to-Coast Walk and was developed by the late A. Wainwright, a famous English naturalist. Wainwright set out to create a walking trail that encompassed the very best England had to offer.

Whenever possible, he followed the paths of 10th-century Viking settlers who wanted to avoid the long sea journey around Scotland to Ireland. The result is a 190-mile route joining the ancient coastal hamlets of St. Bees Head on the Irish Sea with Robin Hood's Bay on the North Sea.

Described as one of the great walks of the world, three-quarters of it passes through three national park districts.

In the west is the ruggedly beautiful and mountainous Lake District, the most challenging yet visually rewarding part of the route.

In the middle is found the rolling hills and meadows of the Yorkshire Dales, the land of James Herriot's "All Creatures Great and Small."

Finally, you enter the haunting loneliness of the windswept North York Moors in the east — mile after mile of misty, heather-covered highlands dotted with ancient burial mounds, Celtic crosses and stone circles.

In between, the trail leads down

miles of public footpaths, over countless stone fences and through dozens of farmyards.

On English soil

I arrived at Heathrow at 10:30 a.m. with a medium-size backpack, comfortable hiking boots, rain gear, route maps, compass and walking stick. I also had an accommodation guide in my pocket listing all possible places to stay along the route.

The subway, or Tube as the locals call it, took me to Euston Station. From there I caught the London-Glasgow train to Carlisle, where I transferred to a tiny coastal train to St. Bees. When I arrived that evening, I was exhausted. Jet lag was taking its toll!

The only lodging I had arranged ahead of time was my first night in St. Bees. The **Outrigg House** was a typical B&B offering a private bedroom, hot bath and huge English breakfast. The cost was £14, or about $22 — average for the trip.

In the days ahead I also stayed in a variety of fascinating youth hostels which were a little cheaper, but with less privacy, and pub-hotels, a little more expensive but very convenient.

Ready to go

The next morning was bright and clear as I headed up the cliff to St. Bees Head, the official starting point of the journey. To the west you could see the Isle of Man. To the north, the hills of Scotland.

I was anxious to get going and hurried down to the water's edge to collect my "official pebble." Tradition dictates that you should carry a pebble with you and toss it into the sea on the other side. I was only hoping I'd make it that far.

Everything I'd read recommended at least 14 days to complete the walk. Unfortunately, I only had 12, which meant I needed to average almost 16 miles a day.

Which way to go?

Hikers constantly debate which direction to walk. Some prefer walking east to west to save the beautiful Lake District for the grand finale. Others recommend walking west to east to benefit from the prevailing westerly winds at your back. This was my choice.

As it turned out, the wind blew in my face the entire trip — but I managed to finish anyway. I had my doubts at times, especially during the first few days of struggling up and down the steep hills of the Lake District. But by the time I reached the halfway point at Keld I knew I would make it all the way.

I did get lost once in the moors. Luckily, it was a clear day and visibility was good. (Quite often in the moors, you are fortunate if you can see 25 feet through the thick mist.)

I kept walking in the right general direction and eventually surprised a couple of local bird-watchers. They put me back on the right path, but the detour added several miles to what was already a long day.

The history, the B&Bs

The entire walk was exhilarating and the scenery unforgettable. But it was the tiny villages with their lovely B&Bs and ancient pubs filled with friendly people that I really enjoyed.

Although I was traveling alone, or "on your own" as the English say, I ran into many of the same walkers every day. The villages were too tiny to have more than one or two pubs and we'd often meet in the evenings to compare blisters and B&Bs.

I recall one B&B in Ingleby Cross that was absolutely amazing. It was called **The Monks' House** and was built in the 1300s! Arriving after a particularly difficult day, I was led to a cozy fire, a pot of hot tea and a generous slice of homemade chocolate cake swimming in a bowl of fresh cream.

The owner was very proud of her home and displayed a list of previous tenants. Many of them were Catholic monks who had died when the Black Death swept through Europe in the 14th century. Just imagine staying in a home almost 700 years old!

But I remembered that in England age is relative. Earlier in the day I had stopped at the hamlet of Bolton-on-Swale where, in St. Mary's churchyard, is buried the famous Henry Jenkins, a local who lived to the ripe old age of 169 years!

Butterlip How Youth Hostel — Grasmere.

The food?

I must compliment the English on their food. I was surprised by the wide and interesting variety I found everywhere I went. Evening meals, usually taken at village pubs, ranged from large bowls of thick, fresh soups to steak and vegetable pies and various kinds of Yorkshire pudding. One evening I had wild boar.

Noon meals consisted of fresh fruit, wholesome breads and a wonderful selection of cheeses bought along the way.

English breakfasts were hearty

enough to last most of the day. They started with juice and cereal served with the inevitable pot of tea, toast and marmalade. Then came a platter covered with two large sausages, a rasher of thick-sliced bacon, eggs, fried tomatoes and grilled mushrooms and/or baked beans on toast.

It took a little getting used to, but I ate every bite, every day. After a breakfast like that, you could walk a long ways.

Mission accomplished

On the 12th day I finally arrived at Robin Hood's Bay around 5 p.m. It had been a long day, almost 20 miles, as I entered the village via a slippery, windswept cliff. I found **Devon House** and the innkeeper rushed me inside, clucking about the "wretched weather" and about my "catching a death of cold."

Setting my pack and walking stick in the corner, I started to take off my rain gear.

"Oh, no," she exclaimed, "you mustn't stop now. Take your pebble to the ocean and throw it in. It's only a wee bit farther. And don't forget to sign the register at **The Bay Hotel** to get your Coast-to-Coast certificate," she admonished.

Properly chastised, I went out again, into the rain and fading light, down what seemed to be the world's longest and steepest cobblestone street, to throw my Irish Sea pebble into the North Sea. Out on the end of a slippery pier, I tossed it into the wind and the waves. There wasn't a soul in sight.

At the foot of the pier stood The Bay Hotel, an ancient stone building leaning slightly out and over the water. I walked up to the door, obediently took off my mud-spattered boots and entered.

Immediately I was met with a round of applause by a group of smiling locals standing around the bar.

"What in the world?" I thought, taken aback with surprise!

But of course, the innkeeper had called ahead and told them an American had come all this way to walk across England and would soon be stopping by. They had been watching for me through the window.

In that instant I knew it had all been worth it: the struggle through the Lake District, splashing my way across the rainy dales and even getting lost in the moors. And I was deeply touched.

They waved me into the smoky room and made space for me by the fireplace.

"Well done, Yank," smiled a weathered old fisherman as he handed me a pint of hand-pumped ale. "Well done!"

The walk was officially over.

Planning your walk

Places to stay

It's hard to find a bad place to stay in England, but here are my favorites:

- **Outrigg House**, St. Bees Head, Cumbria, CA27 0AN; phone 01946-822348 — cost, £14.
- **Royal Oak Hotel**, Rosthwaite, Cumbria, CA12 5XB; phone 017687-77214 — cost, £22.
- **YHA Goldrill House**, Patterdale, Cumbria, CA11 0NW; phone 017684-82394 — cost, £12.
- **YHA Fletcher Hill**, Kirkby Stephen, Cumbria, CA17 4QQ; phone 017683-71793 — cost, £10.
- **Oxnop Hall**, Gunnerside, North Yorkshire, DL11 6JJ; phone

01748-886253 — cost, £21.

• **Monks' House**, Ingleby Cross, North Yorkshire, DL6 3ND; phone 01609-882294 — cost, £14.

• **Horseshoe Hotel**, Egton Bridge, North Yorkshire, YO21 1XE; phone 01947-85245 — cost, £19.

• **Devon House**, Robin Hood's Bay, North Yorkshire, YO22 4RL; phone 01947-880197 — cost, £14.

A complete Coast-to-Coast accommodation guide can be ordered from the Ramblers' Association, 1/5 Wandsworth Rd., London SW8 2XX, England; phone 01715-826878.

The YHA Coast-to-Coast Booking Bureau also can make all arrangements ahead of time. Write YHA Northern Region, P.O. Box 11, Matlock, Derbyshire DE4 2XA, England, or call them any time of day at 01426-939215.

Additional things to see and do along the walk

Visit Dove Cottage in Grasmere, home of poet William Wordsworth. Take the lake steamer across Ullsdale Water in Patterdale. Ride the steam train through the countryside at Kirkby Stephen.

Absolutely necessary gear (any time of year)

Take waterproof, lightweight hiking boots, properly broken in; walking staff; wind- and waterproof jacket and pants; cap or hat; day pack, and water bottle. (During fall months, add a warm sweater, warm stocking cap and gloves.)

Physical condition

As with any other strenuous activity, you should be in good physical condition to enjoy it. The Coast-to-Coast route is 190 miles long and should be considered a serious walk. You should be comfortable walking at least 10 miles a day in hilly countryside, twice that on level ground.

Important information

Wainwright's "Coast-to-Coast Guidebook," $19.95, and "Coast-to-Coast Topo Mapset," $23.90, are both available from Adventurous Traveler Bookstore (phone 800/282-3963).

For those who don't want to carry everything on their back, the Coast-to-Coast Packhorse Service (daily baggage transportation for walkers) can be reached by telephoning England: 015396-23688.

A free brochure, "Britain For Walkers," can be obtained from the British Tourist Authority by calling 800/462-2748.

For additional information, three good websites to check are *www.gorp.com/gorp/activity/europe/britain.htm* or *http://escher.earth.ruu.nl/~keijzer/lopen/ctoc.html* or *www.netlink.co.uk/users/ldnet/*.

Miles of stone fences are no obstacle to hikers.

Britain country walking tours — affordably

PAT SNIDER, Oakland, CA

The slick brochures filled with photos of happy hikers strolling along European country lanes looked very appealing to me, but the $200-$300 daily rate seemed more daunting than the climb to the summit of Pike O'Blisco.

Fortunately, there is a delightful, inexpensive alternative called HF Holidays, a British nonprofit organization that has been arranging hiking holidays for more than 80 years.

Country accommodations

Founded in 1913 with the noble ambition of providing workers in industrial areas with an opportunity to escape to the countryside, HF Holidays offered a week's vacation for a week's wage — a rule of thumb that is still followed.

Their most popular program, Best of Britain, features a week at one of 20 country houses scattered throughout England, Scotland and Wales.

My choice, **Monk Coniston**, was located in the Lake District, near the village of Coniston, just a short taxi ride from Windermere.

The house, a National Trust listed property, featured a spacious lounge, dining room, bar and minstrels' gallery and was surrounded by beautifully landscaped grounds with commanding views of Coniston Water and nearby mountains.

A 17th-century barn provided a venue for dancing and games, and two stone cottages supplemented the main house rooms.

Slaters's Bridge, Little Langdale.

While the accommodations were modest, they were clean and well furnished with linens and teapots and had central heat. Some rooms were en suite (British for private bath), while others shared communal facilities.

The food (all meals included) was excellent. Traditional English breakfasts of porridge, eggs, bacon, sausage, kippers, and baked beans on toast provided more than enough cholesterol and energy for the daily hikes.

Picnic lunches were assembled from a buffet of goodies and included sandwiches of the oddest combinations: tuna and corn, cottage cheese and pineapple, egg and mayo, cheddar and chutney. Dinner, always accompanied by very well-cooked vegetables, offered several selections of starters, entrees and desserts.

Hiking options

Each day featured a choice of three hikes at varying levels of physical challenge. The difficult hikes ranged from nine to 13 miles with ascents of as much as 3,800 feet, while the easy level covered six to nine miles with 800- to 1,300-foot ascents.

Some of the hikes originated at the house, but often bus transportation was provided to the trailhead, thus enabling access to a larger part of the Lake District.

Hikes were described in detail the night before so that selections could be made based on interest and ability.

Having chosen the easy hikes, I found them to be leisurely paced with lots of stops for photographing and shoe tying (my favorite excuses for catching my breath!).

While more rigorous hikes covered the rugged mountaintops, we were content to wander through farms and sheep pastures, down narrow lanes, over stone bridges and fences and through small villages with pub and tea stops en route.

The hike leaders, all trained volunteers, were well versed in local lore, history, flora and fauna and never once got lost.

Warm atmosphere

In the evenings, a variety of homespun activities was planned including barn dancing (no skill necessary), team quizzes, card tournaments and slide shows. While participation was encouraged, there was no pressure to join in.

Of course, the great advantage of this holiday was the opportunity to get to know the British better. While there were a few Americans, Canadians and Germans, most of the hikers came from all over Great Britain.

The atmosphere, established from the very beginning, was convivial and informal, and mixing was always encouraged. By the end of the week, we all felt like old friends.

Arranging a holiday

Brochures are available from HF Holidays, Imperial House, Edgware Road, London NW9 5AL (phone 0181 905 9556, or fax 0181 205 0506). . . or by contacting their U.S. agent, Wilson and Lake International; phone 800/227-5550.

In addition to the Best of Britain program, they also offer hiking tours in Europe and a wide range of special-interest holidays.

Prices, depending on location and time of year, varied from £255 to £355, or approximately $405 to $560, per person sharing twin accommodations (1995). This included seven nights, all meals and guided hikes.

Single rooms and private baths are available for a small additional amount.

Monk Coniston, a National Trust listed building, is one of 20 country homes owned and leased by HF Holidays.

In foreground, part of excavated fort of Housesteads, starting point for walks on Hadrian's Wall.

Hadrian's Wall by bus and afoot

VIVIAN WILDER, San Francisco, CA

Hadrian's Wall was started in 122 A.D. and it is agreed that the Roman Emperor Hadrian did actually order the wall to be built. It was to be Rome's northern frontier and to separate the Romans from the barbarians. The wall was to extend from north of Carlisle to the mouth of the River Tyne in the east.

Busing to the wall

I was in England in August 1994 for the express purpose of visiting and perhaps walking on the wall. As I did not want to drive on the wrong side of the road I planned to walk, and, in doing my research, it appeared that the closest point to the wall was the town of Haltwhistle.

The National Express Bus was the least expensive way to travel there. The senior pass for £7 ($10.50) allowed a 40% discount on all bus tickets. (I was fortunate in planning on the bus as the trains were not running due to strikes by the personnel.)

The tickets from Gatwick, via Heathrow, to Carlisle, Newcastle, York and back to London totaled £42 ($63). Not able to get a bus ticket from Carlisle to Haltwhistle in London, I made arrangements to stay overnight in Carlisle at a B&B (**Langleigh House**, #6 Howard Place, six blocks from the bus station). The cost was £18 ($27) single with private bath and full breakfast.

At arrival in Carlisle I got information on buses to Haltwhistle for the next day (£2, or $3, at noon). Carlisle is a small, bustling town, but the wall is not within walking distance; Haltwhistle is much closer.

Haltwhistle castle find

My choice of lodging for Haltwhistle was Bellister Castle, a renovated small castle. I had no idea of where in Haltwhistle it was. Seeing the signs mentioning Haltwhistle, I asked the bus driver where the castle was and he replied, "Sorry, Love, but I am new to this run."

Luckily, a young person on the bus was familiar with the castle and directed me to the stop closest to it.

I began to walk in the direction given and, as I could not spot anything resembling a castle, I stopped a villager for directions.

He pointed out an old ruin approximately half a mile down the road, over a bridge and in the woods: "That's the castle."

Not having a sleeping bag with me, I was a little concerned but kept on walking.

Behind the ruins there was a delightful little castle, completely renovated and with accommodations for three couples, each with a private bath.

As I am not a couple, my room was the smallest, 20'x30'; my bath had a huge soaking tub, along with the rest of the usual fixtures.

Full breakfast was included and delicious dinners were available for approximately £20 ($30) including wine.

The owner, David Taylor, used to renovate old buildings and fell in love with this castle. After finishing the work, he decided to stay put for a while.

He is an excellent chef and I recommend this place and his cooking highly. He can be reached at Bellister Castle, Haltwhistle Northumberland NE49 ONZ, England; phone 0434-320391.

The wall, at last!

The castle is NOT close to the wall, but in the small town I found the bus (No. 890, Waugh's Coaches) that covers all of the sights that are connected with the wall.

The bus runs from Haltwhistle to Hexham via Milecastle, Once Brewed, Housesteads, Chesters andAcomb and return. The bargain whole-day Rover ticket was £3.80, or $5.70, adult.

My first stop on the bus was Vindolanda Museum, frontier home for some of the Roman soldiers. Set in charming gardens, it had a walk that was listed as three miles to the wall.

After touring the museum I headed out to the walk. The signpost pointed up a grassy knoll, but no path was discernible. I did climb up to the top but couldn't figure out where to go from there. Back down to the museum, I walked out the back of the museum and followed the road that I thought was in the direction of the wall.

As I did not have a compass, I finally stopped one of the few cars and asked for directions; wrong-way me wound up walking back to the museum and catching the bus to Housesteads.

After a long trek up the hill to Housesteads, an excavated fort with a preserved Roman latrine, I finally got a close-up glimpse of the wall.

Housesteads is the starting point for walks on the wall both east and west, but as there was no easy way I could clamber onto the wall I just took pictures and caught the bus back to Haltwhistle.

After the half-mile walk back to the castle, my host prepared dinner for me: scrambled eggs with smoked salmon on toast to start, chicken breast in a honey-mustard sauce with steamed broccoli, potatoes and pea pods, wine and coffee — excellent!

The night was so quiet, in the distance I could hear the soft baaing of sheep and an occasional clop-clop of a horse.

Roman Army Museum

Tuesday, the bus took me to within a half mile of the Roman Army Museum. This museum has displays of Roman objects plus a large-scale model of the fort. A reconstructed barracks room shows a part of the Roman soldier's life.

However, there was no easy access to the wall. So I was off to Hexham, a nice market town where I had lunch (very good fish cakes).

All along the bus route I could now recognize the wall and saw some people walking along the top. The bus passed a point near Hexham where a portion of the wall is readily available to someone with a car. There, the portion is only two feet high; elsewhere, it averages four to six feet high.

Then I was back to the castle for dinner: pork chop with caramelized onions, steamed carrots, green beans and rice, coffee, wine and dessert of hot waffle with ice cream and fresh strawberries. So glad I booked in.

A full day

Wednesday, I caught the bus to Once Brewed and walked up to Steel Rigg. I was able to see and touch the wall and, at last, walk along it for a short while. It is uneven and I am not that surefooted.

I walked back down and took the next bus to Chesters to see the fort, which is extensively excavated, and the museum. There is a huge area with the excavated ruins marked out and signposts listing what each ruin once was — all of this along the Tyne riverside, with flocks of sheep roaming all over as well as tourists.

I had to go into Hexham again to check on the train to Newcastle, which was where I got the bus to York, my next main visit after the wall.

Apparently, the train strikes did not affect the service in Northumberland.

Dinner back at the castle was again delicious with a starter of crisp-broiled fish fillet, celery Stilton cheese soup, steak with bearnaise sauce with steamed zucchini and potatoes as well as coffee and wine. How could I leave?

Touring particulars

My stay in Haltwhistle, searching for the wall, was four days short. The weather (in August) was cool and walking was very invigorating.

Bellister Castle charged £33 ($49.50) a night; the rooms had feather comforters, and terry robes were provided for all visitors.

There is no train station as such at Haltwhistle, just a platform on either side of the tracks, but the trains do stop and tickets can be purchased from the conductor.

I was able to get a 50% reduction on the train fare to Newcastle by using my senior bus pass!

The commander's house near the east gate had an under-floor heating system and a heated bath suite. Beyond the gate are the River Tyne and the excavations of the fort bath house.

Chesters Fort on Hadrian's Wall

LEI CHATFIELD, Senior Editor, ITN

England's mazes are legendary — those perfectly sculpted hedges, showcases in their already perfect gardens. They were meant to be fun. We found that "more fun" is the highway-system maze that leads to one of Britain's ancient sites, Hadrian's Wall.

Approaching by car from Newcastle upon Tyne in the east, we were doing well until we were deluged with fog. We were lucky to see the road, let alone notice any directional signs or any sign of the wall. I was grateful that my husband was the appointed driver.

We finally came out of the fog long enough to find Chesters Fort, the best-preserved Roman cavalry fort in Britain.

This was the highlight of our two visits to the wall. (Later in our trip we approached the wall from Carlisle in the west, once again on A69.)

Exploring the wall

Our approach from the west was more successful. If you have only a short time to see the wall, I'd suggest this route.

Starting at about 15 miles from Carlisle, there are five forts in a short distance, including Chesters and the most visited, Housesteads, which is the best place to walk along the wall. The latter also has a museum, but we didn't find it as interesting as Chesters'.

The wall itself, built from A.D. 122 to 132 under the rule of Hadrian, served as the northwest frontier of the Roman Empire for 300 years.

Punctuating the wall at each mile were small guard posts called milecastles. At more distant intervals were forts that housed the regiments that were assigned to protect the province from northern "barbarians."

The wall originally was up to 10 feet thick in places and 20 feet high. Now the wall is only about six feet tall at its highest points. After the Romans left, the locals considered it a good supply of stone for building houses, churches and field walls; this continued well into the 19th century.

Clayton to the rescue

When John Clayton inherited the Chesters Estate in 1832, he started excavating the grounds of the estate leading to the River Tyne. In the ensuing years he purchased several major Roman sites in the area to preserve them and in his spare time set about excavating the remains of the wall.

He also unearthed and added to his collection relics found at the various sites. These finds were on display for visitors at a garden pavilion on the estate.

After his death in 1890 a museum was built to display these antiquities. Visitors to the museum at Chesters Fort today will see virtually the same display as did visitors after the turn of the century.

The main room of the museum is devoted to sculptures, stone reliefs and miscellaneous artifacts discovered on the various properties. The second room houses a collection of military ironwork.

We visited the museum after exploring the fort and bath house located just outside the fort walls. The museum then gave us a better understanding of what we had seen.

However, the exploration of the site is much more rewarding if you purchase English Heritage's "Chesters Roman Fort" booklet (£1.50) at the small shop at the entrance before you start your tour.

The fort

With guidebook in hand, we approached the fort from the north under the watchful gaze of resident cattle. We found at many places along the wall, with resident cattle and sheep, that it was wise to watch where we stepped.

The fort covers an area of 5.7 acres overlooking the river and gives visitors an idea of the life of the frontier soldiers.

The guidebook suggested turning right and circling the inside of the fort, inspecting its entrance gates before inspecting the major excavations.

Since our time was limited, and fearing the fog might roll back in before we could get photos, we headed forward to the pair of facing barracks blocks, each thought to have housed 64 to 80 men.

Running down the middle of the road between the barracks was a drainage system that would have been covered by stone slabs.

In the center of the fort we found the headquarters building with a partly sunken strong room with a ribbed roof. When excavated in the 1800s, an iron-studded door was still in place.

Beyond the headquarters building toward the river we saw the commander's house, which I found most interesting with its hypo-

View of Chesters Fort's barracks. The street between had a drainage system that would have been covered by stone slabs in Roman times.

caust (under-floor heating system). At the east end was the heated bath suite. The socially advantaged lived a comfortable life even on the frontier.

The fort bath house

Exploration of the site should not stop with the fort, as the extensive ruins of the bath house are located outside the walls, between the minor east gate and the river.

Water fed to the fort by its aqueduct could be diverted to supply the bath complex with water. The waste water then drained down to the river.

The complex was quite sophisticated with a large changing room surrounded by a hot dry room, hot steam room, hot bath, warm rooms, cold bath and a cold plunge.

Down at the river it occasionally is possible to see in the riverbed a bit of the abutment of the bridge that once crossed the Tyne.

Heading back up to the fort, you'll find a fenced portion of Hadrian's Wall.

I found it sad that all the plundering of the wall has left us just a clue of this once-imposing structure. At the same time, I felt fortunate that enough remains and has been excavated to give us a suggestion of the Romans' engineering genius.

Chesters Fort can be found near Chollerford on route B 6318 — even on a foggy day.

American Museum in Britain

LLOYD McCUNE, Contributing Editor

The first museum of Americana outside the United States, the American Museum at Claverton Manor, near Bath, England, was founded by Dallas Pratt and John Judkyn, two Americans whose deep appreciation of American arts led to the establishment of "a museum of decorative arts and of American history, illustrating domestic life in America from Colonial times to the end of the 19th century."

Established in 1961, this museum is set up in a late Georgian house designed by an architect of George IV. The manor contains a series of rooms, many of which are fitted out with the original paneling and floorboards brought from houses in the United States.

These settings are complimented by galleries and exhibits devoted to different aspects of American culture, such as the maritime trade and the opening of the West. Arranged chronologically, domestic scenes form the nucleus of this museum's collection.

There are two separate galleries on the grounds: the New Gallery, which houses David Pratt's distinguished collection of English maps as well as a library containing 7,000 volumes, and a second gallery, housing the museum's folk art collection.

Included in these displays are the crafts of the North American Indian as well as the Spanish settlers of Mexico, plus folk art and quilts, Shaker craftsmanship and 18th-century Colonial furniture.

Claverton Manor is situated on 125 acres of grounds just outside Bath and occupies a prominent position overlooking the River Avon.

Included in these grounds are a Colonial herb garden, a dye-plant border, a replica of George Washington's garden in Mount Vernon and an arboretum established to show the variety of plants and trees that have been adapted to English climate.

Claverton Manor is open each year from March to November. Admission costs £5 (near US$8.20) for adults, £4.50 ($7.40) for senior citizens and students, and £3 ($5) for children. Special visits can be arranged by phoning 01225-460-503 between 9:30 a.m. and 5 p.m.

Clarks of England factory outlet

WALTER K. WORNICK, Alstead, NH

There have been references in editions of ***ITN*** about Clarks shoes, the famous and pricey British shoes.

There is a large factory outlet run by Clarks of England in the town of Street, in Somerset, right on the A-39 near the intersection of the A-361.

The outlet is adjacent to the main factory complex, although many of the shoes are now produced in other countries, such as Portugal, where the pair I purchased was made.

There are numerous stores in the complex and it is beautifully landscaped. Fine chocolates are available, which my British friends appreciate greatly, and fine greeting cards, which are rather costly elsewhere, etc.

There is a store that carries the complete line of Clarks products and then a huge outlet store that has a GREAT selection, if you can find your size.

The staff in the outlet section are very helpful and will measure feet and advise on the correct British size for you. Prices are the best I have ever seen for these shoes. Luggage, etc., is also available.

Take time to visit the free shoe museum next door. While there are masses of shoes there, of interest are the letters and pictures of the Clark family, who built the company.

They were Quakers and used only "slave-free cotton" that was made available through the Quaker churches. They also were opposed to liquor and there are pictures of their parades against pubs in the town.

When shoes began to be produced in America by machines, they visited those factories and marveled at how healthy and well dressed American workers were, as opposed to the workers in their own factories.

I visited in September '96 and stayed at the nearby B&B run by Mrs. L. White (64 Bath Rd., Ashcott, Bridgewater, Somerset TA7 9QJ, England; phone 01458-210256).

The rate was £16 (near US$25) for a single. Ask for a room in the back. There is off-road parking. They also run the Bradley Batch Cactus Nursery, which can be visited and enjoyed on the site.

(VAT refund forms are available at the outlet center for shoes purchased. – Editor)

Touring Britain
CRUISE LOCH LOMOND

Enjoying the Cornish coast is made easier by car.

Driving in Great Britain — it takes 'round about a day to catch on

BILL and SHELLY BLANCHARD, Unalakleet, AK

"Just remember two things," a friend told me about driving in Britain, "stay left and get used to loads of roundabouts."

No kidding!

Actually, after the first day of getting adjusted to using my *left hand* to shift and maneuvering through miles of narrow lanes, the driving became almost routine.

So, why drive?

We spent the month of June 1995 enjoying our first driving trip of Great Britain.

A car was essential, as we enjoy camping at some of the many well-equipped campgrounds all over the country. Needless to say, camping is made considerably easier with a vehicle than by using public transportation.

It pays to shop around

Rates for overseas rental cars fluctuate tremendously; a 3-week quote of $400 could balloon to $550 the next day. Initially, I was sold on the major car companies, but, just for comparison, I called some of the many car-rental consolidators and discovered much lower prices.

We settled for Holiday Autos (800/422-7737), who, through the British car rental company Churchfields, offered a 22-day prepaid rate of $340 including VAT for a Ford Fiesta.

Our plan was to stay with friends near London for a few days and then pick up the car when we were ready to venture out of London.

Picking up the car proved simple enough — just remember to go over the condition of the car and notice *every* little nick and scratch, making sure they are duly noted on the sheet.

Churchfields is located near Heathrow as well as in Hammersmith. When looking for a car in London, remember that the big companies have locations all over the area, so be specific and you may find a better deal in a place other than Gatwick or Heathrow.

Do your homework

The usual rules in renting prevail: the bigger the car, the higher the cost; also, standard transmissions are much cheaper than automatic ones.

For our needs, the Ford Fiesta was the best choice. It was perfect for two people with backpacks and camping gear. The small size made parking easy, gave high gas mileage and helped us to glide through the slender streets. The standard transmission was ideal for the many hills we encountered and contributed to the good gas mileage.

It takes a little while to get used to shifting with the left hand, but the accelerator, brake and clutch are all in the same positions you would find them on a left-hand-drive car.

While in London, I spent some time simply observing the traffic and often would hop on a bus to experience the road safely from a passenger seat. The British Tourist Authority can supply you with simple maps, camping information and motoring itineraries.

Before you start your journey, be sure to pick up a good road atlas of Great Britain. These are widely available in Britain and will run you £6 to £12 (near US$9.60-$19.20), depending on how much detail you want. Often you can find "last year's model" in surplus book stores for £2 or £3 ($3.20-$4.80).

We found the "Ordnance Survey Atlas of Great Britain" superb as it offered good detail and also showed campsites. Each day, before we hit the road, we used a highlighter to mark our route for the day. This helped immensely when looking for the right town or turnoff. It also gave an instant tracking of our journey.

And, you are off!

A driving situation you will come across frequently is when the already narrow two lanes compress to about one and a half lanes. This happens when you enter small towns and cars are parked on one side of the road.

You must correctly gauge the amount of space you have so that you will not hit the parked cars and yet still stay in your lane. It is common to have to jump into the opposite lane if the parked cars take over — you may have to yield, or others will yield for you, when it is impossible for two cars to get through.

Generally, the drivers are courteous and will yield for you. If a car flashes its lights at you, it is a sign that you may advance, not a warning to dim your lights.

Though one can travel many miles in a day, we prefer to move slowly, find a location we like and then stay for at least a few days. For this trip, we concentrated on Wales plus Cornwall and the East Anglia/Cambridgeshire areas.

Campgrounds were easy to locate, especially in Cornwall and Wales. For those of you who need a solid roof over your head, B&Bs are plentiful and most offer a place to park your car. Just look for signs on the road or inquire at the tourist information office.

Highways and byways

Most of the roads you will encounter will be either *motorways*, like our interstates; *A-roads*, which can be 4-lane but usually are 2-lane, and *B-roads*, which are small, paved, 2-lane roads.

The motorways we used were very well maintained. They usually were three lanes on each side and the posted speed limit was 70 mph; however, most folks sped along faster than that.

(In Britain, the slow lane is the far *left* lane — stay there unless you want to pass or are ready to consistently go at 80+ mph in a fast lane.)

As in the United States, there are many of the innocuous and antiseptic roadside stops along the way. These roadside stops include gas stations (usually with higher prices than in town), restaurants, toilets and sometimes even motels a la Best Western or Holiday Inn with rooms for around £35-£40 ($56-$64) per night.

Though they lack any sort of charm, you can be assured of a clean restroom and a quick, fairly inexpensive bite to eat.

A-roads and B-roads vary considerably. Winding, narrow roads are the norm in smaller towns, but this does not dissuade the bus or lorry from making its rounds.

You also may find yourself on one-lane roads in the country. These roads have cutouts to turn into about every 500 yards so that the other car can pass.

Gas stations were in good supply and some were open late at night and on the weekend. To play it safe, we topped our tank often, as we did a lot of traveling in small towns and were unsure of the business hours. Gas prices generally were cheaper at the large supermarkets.

Roundabouts

While stoplights are few and a stop sign is an extreme rarity, their functions are handled by the roundabout.

This can be a stumbling block

The classic British roundabout.

to the average American driver. Your main rule of thumb: remember to yield to the right.

If you are taking the first *spoke* of the roundabout, your car should be in the far left lane — when it is clear, enter the roundabout and make your turn. If you want to go to the last spoke, get into the right lane.

Do not pussyfoot at a roundabout; when you see it is clear, be sure to enter forcefully and keep an eye out for other cars. If you miss your turnoff, just go around again. You probably will curse (or be cursed at!) during the first few you encounter, but with practice you will get better.

Tips, strategies & comments

• Always plan extra time to go places. In midsize and big cities, avoid rush-hour driving from 8 to 9 a.m. and 5 to 6 p.m.

• As in the States, there are many large trucks, or lorries, on the road.

• We saw very few policemen on the road.

• Other than for various toll bridges, all the roads in Britain are free. There is talk, however, that the motorways will become toll roads in the future.

• Have sufficient £1, 50p and 20p coins for parking. Our strategy was to find a car park in the city, pay for a ticket (usually, £1 would go for at least three hours) and not worry about driving around town trying to find a free place on the street.

It appears that the police are very strict about illegal parking. Punishment can range from large fines to having your car towed. We played it safe and parked only where we knew it was legal.

• Sadly, just as in the United States, drinking and driving is a serious problem. While we both enjoy pubs and British ale, we did our best to find campgrounds within walking distance of pubs. If that was not possible, then I nursed a pint along with a good meal to play it safe. I could not take the chance of being under the influence while driving.

• Going solo on a British driving trip would pose little problems, but we found two people traveling together to be ideal. On small, narrow lanes, driving is easier with a partner to help with the atlas and navigation.

• As in the United States, keep the doors locked and remove all valuables when you are away from the car. We had no problems, but almost everyone we met had a horror story of a car break-in. Use common sense.

Returning the car

I recommend leaving early if you are returning the car at Heathrow or Gatwick, and make your drop-off time sometime other than rush hour. At Churchfields, a person went over the "damage" sheet, and we were off. Be sure to ask for a ride to the airport or nearest Tube station.

Conclusion

As teachers, we have to travel during peak season, but the month of June was a great time to travel in England and Wales. Campgrounds were practically empty, B&Bs mostly vacant and restaurants uncrowded.

We hope this article gives those of you who have an urge to try the "other side of the road" the spirit to go for it!

The best way to visit small villages at your own pace is in your own vehicle.

Gritting one's teeth, taking to the road — saying, 'Left, left'

HARLAN HAGUE, Stockton, CA

It's possible to see bits and pieces of the British countryside from the window of a British Rail coach, and it's great fun as well. You can travel in comfort from London to Oxford, for example, then continue your journey to Moreton-in-Marsh in England's north Cotswold Hills.

From Moreton station, it's only one block to the village center with its pleasant shops and tearooms, small restaurants and comfortable hotels. If you arrive on Tuesday, you can wander through one of the best weekly markets in the region.

If you prefer tranquillity to the bustle of the market, take the footpath north of the village toward Bourton-on-the-Hill.

But that's about as far as you will venture from the train station. If you're traveling by rail, you will miss Stow-on-the-Wold, Upper Swell, Lower Slaughter, Bourton-on-the-Water, Shipton-under-Wychwood, Great Tew, Little Compton and Chipping Campden.

To *see* the north Cotswolds, and

indeed rural Britain in general, you must stiffen your back, grit your teeth, rent a car and drive.

Correct left-handedness

Now, most Americans balk at the prospect of driving a car with the steering wheel on the "wrong" side. Many who decide, nevertheless, to give it a try are terrified when they are first poised to enter a flow of traffic streaming down the left side of the road.

Not me. I have lived my life in a right-handed society that only just tolerates left-handers. So I escape as often as I can to a land where the virtues of the left are paramount. The British walk on the left and — bless them — they drive on the left.

It wasn't easy, even for a left-hander, to make the adjustment. Just as my kindergarten teacher tried to persuade me by subtle pressures to adopt the correct right hand, I had to adjust to the correct left-handedness of British driving.

Elated as I was at my first opportunity to enter the rational world of British driving, I was careful. I arranged to pick up my rental car at the most distant Tube stop in north London. I would then, I thought, have a straight shot to the country.

The best plans. . .

Wrong. The rental agency was on the busiest street in north London, which was at the moment of my arrival filled with four lanes of fast-moving traffic. My car was parallel parked at the curb.

I opened the door on the left side, then fumbled in the glove compartment so anyone watching would not think that I had opened the wrong door.

I closed the door and walked around to the driver's side and slipped behind the wheel. I started the engine and tested the brake, accelerator and clutch.

I turned the wheels to the right, raced the engine, found a break in the flow of traffic, let out the clutch to shoot out into the flow and smashed into the van parked directly in front of me. Only then did I see the large fellow sitting at the wheel of the van, which was facing my car.

I reversed the car slowly until I was parked again at the curb. I got out of the car even more slowly. The van driver sat for a moment longer, then got out. We walked together to observe the damage. My car appeared untouched, but I had destroyed his headlight and crushed the side of his grill. We looked at each other.

"First time?" he asked.

I wasn't sure whether he meant "driving in Britain" or "driving."

"Yes," I said.

He smiled, much to my relief.

"Why don't you be on your way, and I'll take care of this." It was the rental agent who had stepped out of his office when he heard the crash. I remembered that just a moment ago in his office I had decided to pay an extra daily fee to add the collision damage waiver. I thanked him.

The large van driver shook my hand, wished me good luck and gave me a pat on the shoulder as I turned to go. The expression "baptism by fire" had new meaning for me.

Turns and roundabouts

Happily, my experience is not a required initiation into British driving. The first thing to remember, and to keep repeating for the first few days, is that the bulk of the car is on the left side of the driver, not the right as in American cars. Keeping that fact in mind will help you remember to drive on the left side of the road.

The most likely place that you will forget is during a turn. If you keep saying to yourself, "Left side, left side," then you should have no trouble in completing the turn on the left side of the street.

Watch out for the roundabouts. This brilliant alternative to the 4-way stop can be confusing until you become familiar with it. First of all, avoid the temptation to speed around the circle counterclockwise. Remember: "Left side, left side."

Stop at the edge of the circle and look right. Traffic already in the roundabout has the right of way. When you see a break, enter the flow slowly, keeping in mind that other vehicles will be trying to edge into the left lane to exit. This is especially important when you are not exiting at the next street.

If others are riding with you, encourage back-seat driving. Passengers are going to be on the edge of their seats anyway, until they begin to have confidence in your left-handed skills. Welcoming their cautions will let them share the learning experience and the terror.

The various roadways

Since your purpose is to see the country, stay off the motorways. Drive the "A" and "B" roads, even the unmarked routes, assuming that you have a detailed local map.

Roads with only one lane, marked "Single Track," are risky. That's *one lane*, not one lane each way. Some locals drive these paved paths as if they were closed racecourses. They can be especially dangerous if high hedges block the view around curves or corners.

British drivers in the countryside tend to be considerate, but the passing places never seem to be in the right place at the right time.

This is not to say that the British are not aggressive. Most "A" and "B" roads have only one lane in each direction. By American standards, the lanes are narrow, and there is usually no shoulder. More often than not, the edge of the road is a cobblestone curb about three inches high.

While tourists of any nationality tend to drive casually, British locals drive fast, follow close enough to read your dash instruments, and pass on hills and curves. Above all else, remember this: if you round a curve and see a car ahead in your lane, coming at you, squeeze *left*, not right.

Off the busy roads, the pace and pulse are slower. The winding lanes between the smaller villages are the least crowded and the most pleasant to drive. It is not unusual to see a car parked in a lay-by or on the verge, with folding chairs and table nearby, spread neatly with a cloth and afternoon tea.

Since you won't likely be so equipped, don't fail to stop in a village tearoom for a nice respite.

At the ready

My family and I stopped beside a narrow lane one day for a picnic lunch. The grass was still moist from an overnight rain, but we found a log at the edge of the wood to sit on and enjoyed our sandwiches and the spring sunshine.

When we finished, we climbed into the car. I started the engine and put the car in gear, but it would not move. The tires simply spun.

I got out and saw that the rear tires had sunk about four inches into the mud. What I had thought was a grassy, hard surface was really a camouflaged quagmire. I tried rocking the car back and forth, stripping gears in both directions. With my wife in the driver's seat, I pushed while she spun the wheels and sprayed mud on my pants.

A car drove up slowly from behind and stopped in the middle of the lane. A man opened the door and stepped out. He was dressed in a neat tweed suit.

"Trouble?" he asked.

Without waiting for a reply, he went to the back of his car, opened the trunk and took out a pair of rubber boots and a shovel. While I watched, he pulled on the boots and came over with the shovel. He dug a few spadefuls from the front of each of the back tires, then filled the cavities with rotted bark and gravel from the roadside.

"Now try it," he said. "Gently."

I tried it, gently, and the car rolled slowly onto the road. I thanked him and pumped his hand.

"Not much you can't do with Wellies and a good shovel," he said.

He pulled off the boots and threw them and the shovel into the back of his car and drove off.

I drove ahead and turned into the "A" road, mumbling, "Left side, left side."

Narrowboat on Shropshire Union Canal

JACQUE J. WEYHE, Juneau, AK

In mid-September '96 my sister and I (seniors) were treated to a wonderful 5-day canal boat outing on the Shropshire Union Canal (Shropshire/Wiltshire/West Midlands area). It was courtesy of my niece and her husband (who live in Bristol), so I am unable to tell you the cost for the four of us.

Our starting point was Norbury Junction, where we were checked out as to how the boat runs, how the locks work, where to take on water, etc., and then we were off **on our own** to negotiate the canal and locks.

All linens, gas, etc., were included; we had only to go to the Safeway Store (no less) in Newport to get our groceries (and, of course, wine) for our big adventure.

The Shropshire Union Canal (SUC) has maximum dimensions for the canal boats: 72 feet long with a 7-foot beam. Our boat, *Grasmere,* steel-hulled, measured 40 feet long and six feet wide, weighed 10 tons and had a maximum speed of four knots per hour on the canal — a wonderfully relaxing pace.

There were four bunks, plus sleeping space for two in the dining area. We had a flush toilet, central heating, hot water, a

"cooker," a fridge and all the cookware and dinnerware needed for our 5-day excursion.

All the villages we visited were beautiful, storybook villages — and we were blessed with very nice weather. We could stop wherever we wished, tie up to the side of the canal and overnight, or whatever. We did have to consider turning around, of course, which was only possible in the occasional "windings" (pronounced like the wind that blows).

We saw cows, sheep, herons, swans, ducks, many, many vine-covered trees, golden leaves falling into the water and dozens of picture-perfect bridges. I took so many pictures that my nephew suggested as a title for my journal "The Bridges of Shropshire County."

At one point on the canal, rather than *under* a bridge we went *over* the road in an aqueduct. We quickly learned to open and close the locks, and each of us had a turn at the tiller.

At the back of a 40-foot boat, aiming the front end through a very narrow opening under a bridge is a bit daunting but not impossible, even for us novices.

At one point we had to negotiate five locks, raising (or lowering, depending upon the direction we were traveling) the boat a total of 33 feet. Talk about photo opportunities!

We did, at one very narrow section of the canal, run aground (and cause the same for several senior ladies moving in the opposite direction). Exciting! Long poles are likewise furnished so you can push yourself off these soft edges.

We visited beautiful villages not found on any of my available maps, such as Brewood (pronounced "brood," which was originally a Roman fort and now is a quiet village with attractive Georgian houses and 13th-century churches), Church Eaton, Gnosall, Wheaton Aston, etc.

At Market Drayton, the largest of the villages we visited, we bought gingerbread. Market Drayton has been the "home of gingerbread" for 280 years, and, as Shakespeare said, "An' I had but one penny in the world thou shouds't have it to buy gingerbread."

We were fortunate to be there for the weekly, 750-year-old street market; we found the tourist office, got a plan of the town and set off to "discover."

In the early 18th century, property taxes were set strictly by the number of windows (openings, not panes); hence, a windowless house was not taxed. We saw some houses where windows had been bricked over and then painted to *look* like windows.

The Shropshire Union Canal was formed under the shadow of railway expansion, the principle being that it would halve the construction costs to lay a railbed along the bed of an existing canal.

By 1849 this plan was abandoned, for the slow development of railways in Wales had shown that canals could still be profitable. Throughout the mid-19th century, SUC remained profitable and was expanded to 213 narrowboats in 1870, 395 in 1889 and 450 by 1902; hence, the canal flourished until WWI.

Another of the larger towns along the canal is Nantwich, a most delightful place with much to see and admire. There was very little that *wasn't* charming, and I cherish the memories of "The Bridges of Shropshire County."

The skinny on narrow boats

TOM & WILMAH DANDO, Alexandria, VA

In September '96 we took a very British holiday by booking back-to-back 7- and 10-day trips aboard a pair of hotel narrow boats owned and operated by Emma and Derek Fearnley, doing business as Inland Waterway Holiday Cruises, Greenham Lock Cottage, London Road, Newbury, Berkshire, RG19 5SN, England; phone 0831-110811.

The boats, *Snipe* and *Tarus,* make a tug-and-tow combination referred to vernacularly as the motor and butty. The butty is cinched up tight against the stern of the motor; even then, a tillerman on the butty is needed to help maneuver.

Each boat is 70 feet long by seven feet wide and flat bottomed, drawing about 30 inches of water. These dimensions and draft are the upper limits that many of the locks and canals will accommodate. On the narrow locks, the boats must be separated and the butty hand hauled through after the motor has locked through.

Speed seldom exceeds three miles per hour, with 10 to 12 miles covered per day. Walking the towpath is the daily activity for most passengers.

Together, the boats accommodate 10 passengers in eight very compact cabins. One cabin has a bathroom en suite; the others have a wash basin with loo and shower

down the hall. The occupants of the en suite cabin said, "Had we known how cramped it was, we would have gladly given up the luxury for more room."

Meals were top flight; however, the highlight of the day was the ritual noon stop at one of the thatch-roofed, stonehouse villages with a pub for a "pint." (It is hard to believe there is such a vast bucolic area in what appears to be a totally developed nation.)

Per diem was just above $110 — a real bargain! Best of all, there was no single supplement.

Canal boats an adventure in Britain

DOROTHY PEAVY, Grass Valley, CA

I would like to add some to the reader's letter "Narrowboat on Shropshire Union Canal." We spent two weeks on the canals of England in 1992 and found it one of our best experiences ever.

There are some 2,000 miles of waterways to pick from. Boats sleep two to 12, with prices starting around $600 in low season. You can rent for a weekend or midweek period, also.

Each is totally equipped except for food, your only additional expense — much like renting a motorhome in the U.S.

Locks are easy to operate, and usually other boaters are around to help. We are both seniors and had never operated a boat but had no problems. The company gives instructions and there are maps to tell every detail of the canals, bridges, locks, villages and canalside pubs and boatyards for water, gas or garbage dropoff.

You meet interesting people and soon feel part of the local scene. We met almost no "foreign" narrowboaters.

Since there are quite a few individual boat companies, it's easiest to work through a company that handles several boatyards.

Richard Batham is the U.S. representative for Blakes (1076 Ash St., Winnetka, IL 60093; phone 800/628-8118, or fax 847/446-4772) and will handle all the details. He will send a catalog of the boats, prices, canals and more. Choosing a boat and canal will entertain you for hours.

The highlight of our trip was going into Wales to Llangollen and crossing the Pontcysyllte Aqueduct, 120 feet above the river and valley. Later, we went through the Harecastle Tunnel (1½ miles). Canals go both over and under roads, motorways and rivers.

You will find that a narrow boat on the English canals is a different experience. Wander leisurely through almost-untraveled countryside exploring tiny villages, or visit places like Oxford, Windsor and the Thames using the boat as your hotel. Docking is free.

Isle of Wight narrow-gauge train steams into Smallbrook Junction from its cross-island run.

Crisscrossing England, Wales, Scotland — Getting mileage out of BritRail Passes

STEVE FISH, Albuquerque, NM

The idea for a British rail vacation sprang from our memories of childhoods crammed with rail travel. Huge machinery roaring past lush landscapes, steel wheels clacking along gleaming tracks, whiffs of diesel and coal fumes: these were sensations we craved all over again.

A self-guided BritRail odyssey last summer brought them back for my wife, Merilyn, and me.

Armchair travel planning

Research was half the fun of our BritRail trip. For months we devoured books.

We found George and LaVerne Ferguson's "Britain by BritRail" to be *the* "how to" reference for self-guiding a rail trip around Britain.

Paul Theroux's "The Kingdom by the Sea" is a rich mosaic of Britain, the cultures and people, drawn by walking and rail-traveling coastal regions, and Susan Allen Toth's "England As You Like It" is a charming "how to" on visiting and enjoying out-of-the-way settings.

We selected baggage that was compact, light, equipped with wheels and stowable pull-handles and rigged so that another bag could be attached piggyback. We practiced schlepping packed piggybacked bags around the house as we would over rail platforms and on and off trains.

Day 1 — shaking jet lag

Aimed at easing jet-lag hassle, we spent our first night in Britain at **Rosemead House** in Horley, Surrey, five minutes' drive from Gatwick Airport. This was our only booked B&B. Our room (£36/$56 with en suite bath) was clean and comfortable, breakfasts were sumptuous and our hosts were fun and friendly.

We also booked the Rosemead for our last night before the return flight home.

Day 2 — Hastings

Our first train left from Gatwick Airport's rail terminal. As we walked, bags trundling behind, our worries faded over getting lost when we saw the easy-to-understand digital train information we were to find posted in stations throughout Britain.

We changed trains at Brighton, then rolled through misty rain along the south channel coast to Hastings.

We inquired about lodging at the rail depot Tourist Information Center, then a taxi drove us over wet, hilly streets to **The Pines** B&B, a pristine Victorian house overlooking Baldslow Road. Our room was spacious and comfortably furnished (£32/$51 en suite).

Clearing skies encouraged walking to most sights, including Hastings Castle and Smugglers' Caves.

English friends picked us up and drove us to their home in East Sussex for Sunday dinner, followed by a drive around East Sussex and a walking tour of Royal Tunbridge Wells.

Days 4-5 — Kent

On Monday morning we rode the train via Ashton to Canterbury, where we lodged at **Ann's House**, a restored B&B on London Road (£38/$62 en suite) providing a nicely furnished but small room and great breakfasts.

We toured Canterbury Cathedral and worshiped at a spirit-lifting choral evensong service.

The following morning, we rode trains to the channel coast to walk around Folkestone and visit Dover for castle and cliff-tunnel tours, then took a cab for a photo stop below the white cliffs.

En route to Portsmouth via London, as we pulled into Maidstone station we realized that Leeds Castle was close by. On impulse, we wrestled bags off the train and toured the sparkling medieval castle.

BritRail's flexible schedules accommodated several bouts of our impulsiveness.

That afternoon, pressing on to London's Victoria Station, we boarded a crowded train to Portsmouth, chatting with a commuting railway employee who regaled us with British rail lore.

Days 6-7 — Portsmouth and the Isle of Wight

Arriving late and tired at Portsmouth, we reluctantly stayed at the **Amberly Guest House** on Castle Road, Southsea (£32/$51 en suite), a run-down facility balanced by its good location for Portsmouth harbor sightseeing.

The next morning we ferried to the Isle of Wight, riding the train from Ryde to Shanklin and back and taking a side trip on the Isle of Wight steam train from Smallbrook to Wootton.

We paused two hours in Shanklin for lunch and a walk in the Old Village, continuing down the Chine historic gorge and along Shanklin Bay's esplanade.

From Portsmouth, we boarded the train north to Hungerford to visit an ancestral manor at Littlecote.

At Reading, we changed to our first high-speed InterCity (IC) train. Settling into our commodious first-class coach, we quickly adjusted to hurtling speeds (up to 140 mph) as the countryside rushed by.

The sparkling rocky Devon and Cornish coastal views en route to Penzance rivaled any seen during the 3-week odyssey.

Days 8-10 — Penzance, Cornwall

The Stanley B&B, perched overlooking Mount's Bay in Penzance, was a lucky find after we arrived late and declined two substandard B&Bs (after Portsmouth, Merilyn insisted, "No more seedy B&Bs!"). Our immaculate room (£36/$58 with shared bath) overlooked a lovely ocean view.

For three days we prowled around Penzance and rode buses to see Land's End and St. Michael's Mount castle.

Days 11-12 — North Wales

An early morning IC train sped us north to Crewe in Cheshire, where we changed to a regional train heading to Llandudno, North Wales.

Due to an overbooking snafu, during two nights we sampled two B&Bs. The **Hollybank**, followed by the **Cliffbury** (both shared bath, £35/$56), were distinguished by tasteful decor and superb breakfasts.

While we enjoyed Llandudno's Victorian charm, our Wales highlight was the Conwy Valley Rail

We visited Leeds Castle after implusively debarking our train at Maidstone, Kent.

Line, linking to the Ffestiniog Railway steam train running through the Snowdonia Mountains from Blaenau Ffestiniog to Porthmadog.

Days 13-17 — Glasgow, Scotland

Leaving Llandudno on the regional train, at Preston we changed to the Scotland-bound IC to Glasgow.

We checked into the **Clifton Hotel** on Great Western Road at Glasgow's West End, a comfortable little Victorian hotel with a huge, ornate room (£34/$54 en suite). Its location was convenient to the underground, city center, museums, Glasgow University and botanical gardens.

We signed on for a Scotguide bus day tour (£15/$24 each) to Loch Lomond, where we took a 90-minute boat excursion (£10/$16 each). We stopped in Inveraray on Loch Fyne for lunch, shopping and a walk around the Duke of Argyll's castle.

Days 18-19 — West Yorkshire

From Glasgow, an IC took us south to Carlisle. We changed to the Yorkshire Dales train for a memorable ride southeast over the lonely moors to Keighley, boarding the Keighley & Worth Valley Railway steam train to Haworth.

Our two nights in Haworth were spent at the **Apothecary Guest House** (£38/$61 en suite) overlooking cobbled Main Street and the valley below.

We agreed that Haworth was the jewel of our Britain tour because we love Brontë literature and lore and fell in love with the Yorkshire countryside and ambience.

We toured the Brontë Museum and trekked the moors to Top Withens, supposed setting for Emily Brontë's "Wuthering Heights."

Day 20 — London, Gatwick and home

We were already gripped by nostalgia as our rail circuit carried us back to London, Horley and Rosemead House for our last night's lodging before our host drove us to Gatwick for our morning flight home to Albuquerque.

For us, rail touring Britain gave us all we wanted and more. We're already planning future rail trips.

Months after returning home, I often lapse into reverie, recalling those clicking wheels and locomotive essences, flashing me back to Scottish lochs, Yorkshire moors and Cornish coasts.

BritRail travel tips

- International air carriers operate in and out of London's Heathrow and Gatwick airports, but travelers may find bargain fares to lesser-used airports around England and Scotland. Joining the British rail system from any airport presents no problem.
- For BritRail Passes, see your travel agent, or contact BritRail Travel International, 1500 Broadway, New York, NY 10036; phone 800/677-8585 or internet *www.britrail.co.uk*. You must purchase BritRail Passes before arriving in Britain. We opted for senior first-class passes at $565 each for 22 days.
- Although private steam train lines don't accept BritRail Passes,

Steam engine at Keighley, West Yorkshire, awaits boarding for Haworth.

don't miss the opportunity to slide back a century by riding these rail relics. Fares are a modest few pounds per person (our experience, tops was £9/$14 per senior on the Ffestiniog; other trains were less).

• For British travel information, write the British Tourist Authority, 551 Fifth Ave., Ste. 701, New York, NY 10176-0799, or call 800/ 462-2748. Outline your travel plans and modes of travel.

• For us, booking B&Bs wasn't necessary in June, but it depends on the time of year and your risk tolerance. We used local tourist information centers which can book B&Bs to your specifications from lists of lodgings held to high standards.

We also referred to Stilwell's "Britain Bed & Breakfast 1996." We found plenty of B&Bs within walking distance or a short taxi ride from most rail depots.

FDR, Ted Lewis and Winston Churchill — London.

Shoestring spring fling to England & Scotland

THEODORE E. LEWIS, Severna Park, MD

June was just around the corner; students would be out of school and the horde of tourists would be taking over Europe. Now was the time to get in a brief trip — before the onslaught began!

All's well. . .

I checked the IAATC (International Association of Air Travel Couriers) fax-on-demand for the last-minute courier flights and noted that Jupiter Air in New York had a 12-day trip to London leaving on May 30 for $150. That was about a week away.

Phoning Marilyn, the courier coordinator, I signed up and was told to meet their representative at the American Airlines counter at JFK at 6 p.m.

Using the Senior Flying Passport I purchase yearly from Continental Airlines, I flew to Newark from my home in Maryland, took an Olympic Bus ($7) to New York City, then a Carey Airport bus ($4 senior fare) to JFK.

The Jupiter representative was late, arriving about 30 minutes prior to departure. He handed me a small envelope, my ticket and instructions, then bade me "Bon voyage," leaving me to check myself in at the counter.

The A.A. counter representative looked at my ticket, pulled my name up on the computer and then said the flight was full and there was no seat for me.

At this turn of events I took umbrage. Several hours earlier I had spoken to another A.A. employee and had reserved seat 28-C on the aisle, not wanting to be wedged between two other passengers.

I told the counter representative that there had better be a seat for me or there would be the devil to pay when the Jupiter shipment arrived at Heathrow without a "warm body" to allow them to clear the shipment through Customs!

She then returned my ticket to me and told me to rush to the departure gate!

Arriving there, the same story repeated itself, but the check-in representative told me to go sit down and she would sort things out. Within two minutes she came running over to me and blurted out, "I've upgraded you to business class. Hurry on board!"

I thanked her profusely, pointing out that it was Memorial Day, and I guessed this was a bonus for being a veteran of WWII! All's well that ends well!

At the other end

Arriving at Heathrow, I went through Customs and Immigration, then proceeded to building No. 139, which was about a block away, where I met Bob, the Jupiter representative.

He took the small white envelope that I was delivering, along with my return ticket, and told me to phone Claire three days prior to my departure date. I was to be at the American Airlines counter and at that time I would get my return ticket and instructions.

My plan was to see Scotland, since I had never been there. Back home I had arranged for an Alamo rental car, which cost me $180 for the week. This included a $30 drop-off charge, since I planned to leave the car in Edinburgh and return to London by train.

On the road

Driving on the left usually makes me nervous the first day, but on this trip I felt right at home. Perhaps serenity comes with old age.

My first two nights were spent with friends in the small village of Mursley, which is about an hour northwest of London. The next night was spent with other friends at their manor home in the Lake Country near Lake Windermere, just south of the Scottish border.

Early the following morning I headed north on M6, passing by Hadrian's Wall, then proceeded over the border into the land of Robert Burns, Bonnie Prince Charlie and "Brigadoon."

Seeing a sign for the town of Lockerbie rang a bell. In December 1988, Pan Am flight 103 had been sabotaged by terrorists and crashed there, killing over 200 people.

One of the victims had been a classmate of my son in elementary school. I stopped in a florist shop for directions and bought a large red carnation, then went to the cemetery and memorial garden. With a lump in my throat, thinking of all those innocent people who had perished so tragically, I left the flower by her name on the marble memorial wall.

I bypassed Glasgow, going on instead to see Loch Lomond. I spent the night at Oban, which is a port with ferries to the Western Isles.

My bed that night was a far cry

from the manor house of the previous night. I checked into a youth hostel ($15) and shared a dormitory with nine other shoestring travelers.

On to Edinburgh

The next day was spent sightseeing: Loch Ness (no, I didn't see Nessie), the battlefield at Culloden and Inverness. That evening was spent in another youth hostel in Pitlochry, said to be the center of Scotland.

I headed for Blair Castle the following morning, then went on to tour the largest Scotch distillery in the Highlands. Yes, you do get a sample, but only a dram!

Though I'm not a golfer, many of my friends are, so St. Andrews was a must. I settled for the 19th hole. That evening I arrived in Edinburgh and again checked into a youth hostel in the center of the city.

I spent the next day sightseeing: I would recommend taking one of the bus tours that allow you to get on and off as many times as you wish.

I made the complete circuit, which takes about 50 minutes, then repeated the course stopping at Edinburgh Castle, which consumed about 2½ hours to see the various museums, the memorial and a good view of the entire city.

Next I walked down the Royal Mile, stopping at various points of interest (the house of John Knox, etc.).

More cost-cutters

The following morning I turned in the Alamo car and then went to the train station where I signed up for a Senior Rail Card. Although it costs £16 ($26) a year, it still saved me money for the one-way fare to London. Using the senior card I paid $73 (plus the cost of the card) instead of $120 — a *total* savings of $21.

The famous Bobby's Bar in Edinburgh.

After a 4½-hour trip I arrived in London, where I purchased a weekend bus/Tube pass for about $6 and good for Saturday and Sunday.

London is one of the most expensive places to stay, but I have found that any ex-serviceman is welcome to stay at the **Union Jack Club** (Sandell Street, London SE1 8UJ; phone advanced reservations direct line, 0171-928-4814, or fax 0171-620-0565).

It is situated right across the street from Waterloo train station. You only have to show a copy of your discharge and you become a temporary honorary member.

Since I am used to youth hostels, I opted for a single room with wash basin and the "loo" down the hall (£25.40, or $39). Rooms en suite are a little more, and families are welcome. There is a restaurant and I've heard many a great WWII story in the pub on the ground floor.

My three days in London were spent window-shopping, seeing a couple of musicals (half-price tickets at Leicester Square), visiting museums and browsing at the antique market on Portobello Road on Saturday morning.

On Sunday I headed for Westminster Abbey for the 10 a.m. service, which has a grand choir. My seat was right next to Ben Jonson — the only person to be buried standing up in that hallowed edifice.

While listening to the choir I thought of my trip to Scotland and what Dr. Samuel Johnson had said after he had made a similar journey to the Western Isles with his traveling companion, Boswell: "Regions mountainous and wild. Thinly inhabited, and little cultivation. . . and he that has never seen them, must live unacquainted with much of nature."

Up-and-coming artists

I always try to be in London on a Sunday. To most people this is a lost day because the stores are closed and the museums don't open until noon, but to me it is the day when struggling artists display their work on the fence at Green Park off of Piccadilly.

Over the years I have purchased a number of paintings from promising artists.

About 18 years ago I purchased an oil for $50 from a fellow named Roy Petley. On this trip I talked to some of the artists and they directed me to his agent the following day. My painting would now sell for about $4,000!

So, if you are in London on a Sunday and you like art, by all means take a walk by Green Park and perhaps you too will have a good eye for an up-and-coming artist.

Sometimes you win. . .

On Tuesday morning I was to meet Bob, the Jupiter representative, at the American Airlines counter in Heathrow at 6 a.m. (an ungodly hour to get to that airport because the buses and trains don't start until about that time).

I solved the problem by taking a taxi from the Union Jack Club to Trafalgar Square, where I got the night bus N-69 to Heathrow, arriving in about an hour.

My flight was only half full, giving me three seats on which to stretch out. Seven hours later I arrived at JFK and met the Jupiter representative, who took the envelope.

Then things went awry — nine

hours from JFK to Baltimore! Thunderstorms made us sit on the tarmac at Newark Airport for four hours!

But, all in all, I had another great courier trip under my belt.

If you would like to give courier travel a go, contact IAATC, P.O. Box 1349, Lake Worth, FL 33460-3742; phone 561/582-8320.

Ruins of the Stone-Age settlement of Skara Brae on the Orkney Islands.

Britain's outer isles

BARBARA KINGSLEY, St. Augustine, FL

In August 1995 I visited what was termed "The Outer Isles of Britain," but the cruise actually included many more ports of call: Dublin, Ireland, then across to Holyhead, Wales, then south to the Scilly Isles and on to two of the Channel Islands, Guernsey and Sark.

Additionally, I elected to go on a pre-cruise trip to Edinburgh for two days, principally to see the Military Tattoo, which might be called a "gathering of the clans." Spectacular is the only word to use, particularly with the castle in the background lit up by torches and with the various clans in their full-dress kilt attire, their bagpipes reverberating.

I elected to go on all the shore excursions, with the exception of the Scilly Isles, where I previously had spent two weeks. What is very interesting about the Scilly Isles, however, is the fact that visitors are limited in number to 2,000 at one time — at least, that was the case when I was there before.

Also, the Tresco Abbey garden there is just gorgeous, with an astonishing variety of subtropical and exotic plants and shrubs from different continents all thriving in the Isle of Scilly's mild climate.

Scottish isles

There seem to be dozens of islands comprising the Scottish Hebrides, many of them uninhabited, but we did get to see the Orkney Islands, where there is a Stone Age settlement called Skara Brae which existed some 5,000 years ago.

It appears that, while it was still occupied, it was suddenly overwhelmed by sand and remained covered for about 4,000 years until it was revealed by a storm in 1850.

The most remarkable features of the village are signs of domesticity such as cupboards, beds, covered passages and open courtyards.

We then went on to the Isle of Harris, where the famous tweed is loomed and where we saw one of the looms in use.

Next, near Stornoway on the Isle of Lewis, we saw one of the most complete prehistoric sites in Britain. The Callanish Stones are laid out in a Celtic cross, with a burial cairn at the entrance. The central pillar casts its shadow exactly along the entrance into the grave at sunset on days of the equinox.

Then came Dunvegan, Isle of Skye; Dunvegan Castle has been the seat of the chiefs of the clan MacLeod for nearly 800 years.

Isle of Man

After visiting Mull and Iona, we called at Douglas, Isle of Man. The scenic drive to Castle Rushen can only be described as enough to take one's breath away, with the gorse- and heather-clad hills and wooded glens riven by bubbling brooks.

The medieval fortress of Castle Rushen was home to the Norse kings until 1265. It was presented to the Manx people by George V in 1929.

The well-known Three Legs of Man appear on the official Manx flag and just why they were adopted is not known, but the favorite local story is that under any circumstances the Manx people always land on their feet!

Ireland and Wales

Our next port of call was Dublin, where we visited Trinity College and saw the Book of Kells. We then continued on to St. Patrick's Cathedral and found out, much to the surprise of many of us, that its denomination is Episcopal.

Also, somewhat surprisingly to some of us, the economy seemed to be very sound, with unemployment down to around 2% and inflation about the same. Dublin is a lovely, bustling city.

From Holyhead, Wales, we took an excursion to Conwy Castle, one of the most picturesque of all Welsh fortresses, and then to Caernarfon Castle. This castle is very impressive-looking and is the most popular attraction in Wales; it also is where the Investiture of the Prince of Wales takes place.

Back to the outer isles

After the Scilly Isles we visited Guernsey, where the scenery is magnificent and the gardens of the individual houses are spectacular.

Our last port of call was Sark, also in the Channel Islands, where there is little wheeled traffic except for horse-drawn carts, which mostly are used for transporting visitors. There are only 600 inhabitants and many of them use bicycles — it's just that no cars are allowed on the island. The islanders are somewhat taciturn but readily give information when asked.

Arranging the trip

This trip was arranged by Lifelong Learning, with whom I have traveled for many years. They are perfection personified, with everybody's itinerary individually prepared and not a detail omitted.

It's run by Jules and Janet Diebenow and they can be reached at 101 Columbia, Ste. 150, Aliso Viejo, CA 92656; phone 800/854-4080, or fax 949/362-2075. They have an extremely efficient organization, and doing business with them is a pleasant experience — particularly these days!

We sailed on the MS *Explorer*, a 94-passenger ship built especially for such trips as this one and also for the Arctic and Antarctic. It was very comfortable, with wonderful food and everybody eager to please.

The mild weather was quite unexpected and nearly everybody on board had packed the wrong clothes!

The trip was in August, but the Scottish Hebrides and Scotland itself are not known for particularly warm weather. In Edinburgh the temperature was 80°F, and throughout the trip the high temperatures caught everybody unawares. There was only one really bad day, though not too awful — just windy and rainy.

The total cost of the trip, including airfare and all meals, was $4,605 and I paid an extra $694 for the 2-day Edinburgh supplement, which included admission to the Tattoo. It was worth every penny.

Welsh tongue twister

As an amusing footnote, I would like to add, particularly for those of Welsh extraction, how the longest word in Welsh Gaelic is spelled. It is Llanfairpwllgwyngyllgogerychwyrndrobwlllantysiliogogogoch and it means "St. Mary's Church in the Hollow Near the White Hazel by the Rapid Whirlpool of the Red Cave of St. Tysilio."

The longest Welsh Gaelic word is displayed here.

Self-navigated narrowboat adventure on Shropshire Union & Llangollen canals

KATHY GIRE, Loomis, CA

The rain dripped off my yellow slicker hood and found a second target on my deck shoes. The shoes made lovely squishing sounds as I hauled myself up on the bow of the narrowboat.

I sighted down the 50-foot roof and caught my husband's eye. He was standing on the stern deck, manning the tiller as he steered us up the Shropshire Union Canal in England; he, too, was barely recognizable as he was totally enveloped in a similar slicker. Only part of his face peeked out.

"Are we having fun yet?" I shouted at him. He flashed me a thumbs-up sign and a big grin, and we both knew that, despite the vicissitudes of the weather, we *were* having fun!

Planning considerations

Our adventure had begun the year before with a casual discussion with some British friends.

We try to visit the United Kingdom each fall to see friends and explore different parts of Britain. Of six families whom we visit, two had expressed interest in trying the narrowboat adventure. One of these couples had actually had the experience several years previ-

(left) The Anglowelsh Base at Bunbury. Ray and Myron pick up the navigational chart. Note the old printing on the building from when the railways operated the canals.

ously, so we relied on them for details.

I did most of the preliminary research on the Internet and had several of the commercial boat hire companies, most of whom have websites, send brochures to all of us. Once we had decided on the time frame, location and specific company, we left the details to our British friends who handled things locally.

We selected what was advertised as a "picturesque route" with a moderate number of locks to navigate in an area we had not yet seen. Think of narrowboating as closer to camping than to cruising, and if you expect someone to bring you "elevensies," forget it.

And they are called "narrowboats" for a reason: our boat was 56 feet long and barely over 6½ feet wide. Boats can accommodate from two to 12 people, all of whom have become very close friends by the terminus of the trip.

Boats are fully equipped with linens, kitchen necessities excluding food, a TV (which we declined) and that ever-important tool, the lock crank key. If you dislike housework, rent a larger boat than you need so you need not make up beds back into dining areas every day.

Most hires are for one week, and you can choose whether to do a return trip using the same route or use a circle canal.

Longer hires are possible, of course, and summer is the peak season and reservations must be made far in advance. We chose an off-season time, late September; we knew we were sacrificing some hours of daylight and assuming the possibility of some "iffy" weather for a chance to see the canals in their uncrowded, natural state.

We chose the Anglowelsh fleet and specifically the Shropshire Union and Llangollen canals. (You can practice your Welsh by trying to pronounce "Llangollen" correctly: THLAN-GOT-THEN). This 49-mile route from Bunbury in Cheshire to Llangollen, Wales, has 56 locks each way and promised extraordinary scenery plus the experience of traversing (twice) the world-famous Pontcysyllte Aqueduct.

Waterways then and now

We and the two other couples, who knew us but not each other, all met in the Cheshire city of Nantwich at the 14th-century **Crown Hotel**. We had lunch there and drove the few miles to the Anglowelsh base at Bunbury trying not to notice the ever-darkening clouds. No few raindrops could dampen the enthusiasm of this crowd!

The first glimpse of our boat, *Solway*, left us only a little disappointed that it was not painted red and green and decorated with the peculiar "rose and castle" design that we had glimpsed so often on previous visits.

The important thing was that we were about to join the ranks of some 4,000 boat crews that enjoy these canals each year.

Early Britons used their rivers as water highways, but the Romans built the first man-made canal. This Fosdyke Canal was used for navigation and drainage. After the Romans departed, canals did not become important until centuries later when came a demand to move huge quantities of heavy stone for building castles and churches.

Throughout the Middle Ages, commerce and river trade gradually increased the transport of building materials. Later in the 18th century, when horse-drawn portage of coal became unsuitable during the muddy winter months, canal use became a real possibility.

The canals had to be hand dug and the men who worked them were called "navvies." They worked according to instructions from an engineer, and during the time from George III to Queen Victoria some 4,000 miles of canals emerged, transforming Britain from an agricultural society to one based on manufactured goods.

The canals reigned supreme until rail transport rendered them obsolete.

The railways systematically undercut the prices of the boatmen and gradually took over control. In 1948, the waterways, many of which had fallen into great disrepair, were nationalized and British Waterways took over management. It was not until the 1960s when people began to experience more leisure time and money that private narrowboats began to appear on the canals.

Restoration groups formed and public support poured in. Repairs began and locks were refurbished and strengthened. From the Industrial Revolution to the Holiday Explosion, the canals have persevered.

Getting started

We checked in at the Bunbury Base of Anglowelsh and got our short steering and maintenance course. Safety was a big issue, as well as rules of the road, so to speak. (The Brits drive on the left but steer their boats on the right!)

We noticed the old printing still visible on the brick canal building that announced "Shropshire Union Railway and Canal Co," a reminder of when the railroads ran the show.

We cast off at 5 p.m. for the short hop before we would have to tie up for the night. Boats operate only during daylight hours, so since we were there in the fall, we had only about two hours of daylight left.

We had purchased a chart and the boatman's bible, J.M. Pearson and Son, Ltd's., "Canal Companion." This small book describes almost every mile of the route, designating all the bridges and locks, giving tips on where to buy supplies and groceries and listing local shops and pubs. It is an invaluable tool while you are on the water and a treasured souvenir afterward.

Leaving the dock at Bunbury put us immediately into the first two locks, and our crew was awkward at first. We had to fumble some to get the lock key into the hole and turn it properly while another helper pushed the heavy lock gate open. The basic rules of consideration apply here, too: leave gates as you find them, so we had to reverse the process as we left.

We were climbing up now, so we entered an empty chamber, closed the lock gate behind us and waited for the water to rush in and raise our level. Whoever is steering has an important job to keep the bow and stern from becoming caught on the gates. It is not difficult but takes some practice.

Steer to the right and *slow down* when passing other boats, especially those that are moored. Average canal speed is only three to four miles per hour, but a speeding 4-mph boat can really wreak havoc on a boat tied up to shore.

Later on in the trip, we obviously irritated a Scottish gentleman who came roaring up on his deck and shouted, "Are ye pullin' a skier behind?"

We got the message.

First mooring

We moored the first night right outside the **Barbridge Inn**, a modern pub that serves canal and road travelers. Our general plan was to fix breakfast on board, eat most lunches there too and buy dinner at the pubs.

This pub was doing a tremendous business, most probably because the food was good and inexpensive, and it was so close to the Bunbury base that boaters just starting out stopped there for the night and boaters returning to base the next day at 9 a.m. had only an hour to go.

The sleeping arrangements on our boat worked out with one couple taking the dinette table down and making it into a double bed. Another couple slept in a double bed that during the day was a long couch in midship.

My husband and I slept in bunk beds in the tapered bow of the boat. I chose the bottom bunk, which could not have been any wider than 14 inches. We were given duvets to roll up in instead of sheets and blankets, and in my case I found it necessary to get out of bed (not an easy task since it was so low to the ground) several times a night just because I felt so confined. My head clearance was also about 14 inches, so nothing could be done in a hurry.

We had two toilets and one shower in a shortened tub for bathing.

We carried a 100-gallon water tank on board, so it was necessary to ration the showers and to replace the water nearly every day. That was not a problem, however, because water hoses and faucets were marked on the charts. There was enough water to handle two showers a day, normal flushing and doing breakfast dishes.

This gave me a chuckle. I got to thinking that in the U.S., we would use paper plates and cups and probably plastic silverware, littering the dumping barrels with all our trash. Our English friends would rather go to the extra bother of "washing up" and not deal with the remains.

On to Llangollen Canal

On day two we got underway at 8:30 a.m. after a "full English breakfast" (fried eggs, undercooked bacon, fried bread, tomatoes, baked beans and mushrooms) cooked by one of our gentlemen. This morning we had a tiller *girl*; narrowboating is an equal-opportunity employer and everyone got a chance to steer, wash up and be a lock monkey.

The clouds were ominous and getting worse, but no one wanted to jinx the situation by mentioning it. At one point or another, however, we all went below and got out our "waterproofs," just in case.

We left the Shropshire Canal with a sharp right turn at Hurleston, a 4-stepping-stone lock that lifted us 34 feet.

There is a reservoir here that contains waters that have come down from the headwaters of the River Dee in Wales, our ultimate destination. Fortunately for all who use the canals now, if it were not for this natural water channel, this canal would have been abandoned during World War II.

We were now on the Llangollen Canal, and the bridges were beginning their numbering with "#1." Our "Canal Companion" told us that the original canal mappers never had this route in mind but that it had just evolved.

Seeing the towpath that runs along almost every foot of the canals reminded us of the first power provided to the canal boats. Horses and sometimes mules and donkeys pulled the heavily laden commercial loads, and we were intrigued to see at various points old brick stable buildings that were home to the canal horses. When speed was a factor, there were boats called "fly boats" that could "fly" through the canals with very fast horses.

As we passed through bucolic countryside, sometimes populated with cattle and horses, we remarked on how little this scene must have changed in the last several hundred years.

British ambiance

Our luck ran out, and down came the torrents of rain. "Washing up" was the preferred inside job, but we still took turns steering and being the lock monkeys. Our waterproof pants and hooded slickers worked well, and we all had sturdy deck shoes.

We had one among us who had done a narrowboat adventure before and we left it to him to plot our daily course using the time parameters of one week. We had so many miles to make each day, so unless the rain became so heavy that we could not safely see, we continued on.

The canal widens and narrows in spots, and it has become overgrown with vegetation in others.

When the rain ceased, nature treated us to a lovely rainbow, and I took my turn at the tiller. It was tricky business getting used to the long response time between a turn from your hand and a reaction from the boat. Most of us took a couple of good cracks against the bank before we got the routine mastered.

Wet shoes and clothes hung out on every nail and splinter. When the wind whipped up, our friend Sue, just recently retired from British Airways, used her airline "footsies" (socks) as gloves and we kept warm water in the sink for thawing out frozen fingers. Fortunately, my husband and I had brought gloves.

But. . . we were having a grand time, and warm British beer just added to the ambiance!

Wrenbury

At Wrenbury we were disappointed not to have to use a special key given us for just this lock. The key activates a mechanism that closes a bridge against the road traffic so that boats can cross through the canal. The preceding boat had already done the honors and waved us through — a prime example of canal courtesy.

This bridge had been restored in its original manner and the old warehouses along the water's edge sported new brick.

Wrenbury is home to a couple of wonderful pubs and a store that sells everything from groceries to artwork. We laughed at a mug that proclaimed, "I did NOT fall into the Llangollen Canal," but we should have been more circumspect in light of what happened a few days later.

Wrenbury is also the base for the Alvechurch Narrowboat Company, and that fleet is all painted in the traditional red and green colors.

The painting and artwork on the canal boats have a long and interesting history. The first decorations on the boats must have been purely functional with symbols and letters for easy recognition. When the boatmen began living aboard their boats, and especially if they had their families with them, then more colorful outside decorations appeared.

Because space was so very limited inside, decorations outside took the place of bric-a-brac and inside art. The stylized form of decoration is called "roses and castles" and probably began in the late 19th century. Roses were very popular, as were romantic castles, and this became a living art form for over 100 years.

It was a style that artisans could do quickly, as time was money for the boatmen. Most boatyards employed at least one artist, and styles varied from north to south.

An evening in

Bright sun greeted us past Wrenbury and lasted for almost two hours. At about 3 p.m. we passed through Marbury whose church gate celebrates "Ye who live mid English pastures green." And green they were, and glistening from the recent rain. We were passing the end of the Sandstone

On the Pontcysyllte Aqueduct.

Trail, a lovely walking trail that stretches from there north along the Cheshire Ridge to Beacon Hill.

In a deluge, the very one chronicled in the opening paragraph, we approached Grindley Brook locks, a series of six locks, three of which are close enough to be considered "staircase." A splendid old lockkeeper's house was barely visible through the downpour, but I made a note to try to get a look at it when we came back this way, hopefully next time in sunshine.

Our British Air friends, Terry and Sue, decided to do a little shopping and came back with two new waterproof rain suits — and gloves.

During the busy season, these locks can cause considerable delays, up to three hours. In heavy traffic, the usual protocol of "one boat up, one boat down" is abandoned and a more practical "three up and three down" takes over. This maximizes water usage since these locks lift you up or down some 40 feet.

At Whitchurch Arm of the canal we tied up to reconnoiter and see if we could spot a pub for dinner. We played some games and began the English tradition of "tiffin" (drinks). According to our charts, we were not even close to a town. The darkness was settling in and the rain torrential.

We made dinner from available supplies: bacon, eggs, baked beans, tuna, cucumbers and cheese. We felt like adventurers cut off from civilization — Shropshire Family Robinsons — and had a rousing game of Trivial Pursuit, British version, until Morpheus felled us all.

Change of scenery

The next morning I thought I was home and being awakened by our horses. Instead, as I sat up too quickly and took a good bash in the forehead, I found that we had tied up just outside a stable and the local resident was peering at us in hopes of feed.

The sun was bright and the air fresh. We headed back to the main canal searching for a water tank and wondered what Welsh "oggies" might be. They were certainly highly touted in the chart book. We decided finally they had to be akin to Cornish pasties.

Whitchurch, we read, is famous for cheese and clocks, but the pastoral scenery is timeless and peaceful and reminded me of the land of "The Wind in the Willows." I fully expected Toad Hall to swing into view around the next bend.

Somewhere here, we slipped across the Welsh border, but no sign announced the change. This was Clwyd, once known as Flintshire. Many lift bridges kept us busy; others are fixed upright so that local farmers can lower them to cross livestock from one side of the canal to the other.

Just as quickly, we slipped back into England. The border here is somewhat nebulous. We had to wait until we crossed the much-anticipated aqueduct before we would be in Wales again.

We filled our water tank and became aware of a subtle change in the scenery. Peat moss was everywhere, coloring the landscape with brown and silver. Many people migrated here in the 18th century when the Enclosure Movement displaced peasants.

Crops do not survive here, but peat does, and it is commercially cultivated. The mosses gave an eerie aura to the countryside, and the memory of it stayed with us.

Ellesmere

At Wixhall Moss, we went ashore for milk and other perishables and ended up buying gloves for assorted cold hands. The rains came again but did not stay long. It was now my turn to drive, and it was difficult to take into account the wind, current, speed and response time of the boat. I realized then that I was probably much better at "washing up" than steering.

The Ellesmere Tunnel loomed ahead. This was our first tunnel and we were eager to do it right.

This is a one-way proposition, so we turned on our headlight and sounded the horn. No answering horn or single eye, so the way must be clear.

In we went. First in has the right of way. Fortunately, we met no other boats, and in a very strong wind but bright sun we slipped into a mooring spot among some 50 other boats at the boatyard in Ellesmere.

Ellesmere traces its history back to the Iron Age, but it has primarily thrived on agriculture. Original maps called this the Ellesmere Canal, an ambitious attempt to link the rivers Mersey, Dee and Severn with a main line from Chester.

When it became apparent that this would never happen, the canal joined with the Chester Canal and the new Birmingham and Liverpool Junction Canal to form the Shropshire Union Railways and Canal Company.

The Llangollen Canal was then simply called the "Welsh" section and did not emerge until a 1956 British Waterways cruising book was published.

Ellesmere became the headquarters for the new company and built offices there. These buildings are now private residences and the British Waterways Border Counties Maintenance Depot headquarters here. The pleasant town caters to canal travelers who often choose to moor overnight.

"Mere" means lake, and there are seven of them in the area formed as the great glaciers retreated during the Ice Age. They are now home to many species of birds, including kingfishers that we saw along the canal.

Walking back to our boat, we struck up a conversation with a couple in a lovely red and green boat who were obviously living on board. They graciously gave us a tour and told us they are on the canal all the good months and only hole up for the harsh winter season.

In occasional shops along the way, we were struck by postcards and artwork depicting the boats laden with snow making their way along the icy canals. We could hardly imagine anything colder.

Canal-boat peculiarities

We passed the Frankton Locks, which necessitated a sharp left turn and a few scrapes along passing boats, and got our first good look at "canalia." "Canalia" consists of the decorative pieces of ironwork permanently fastened to the roofs of the boats.

We saw large, cast-iron pitchers, flowerpots and buckets, all decorated in the "rose and castle" motif. Now they are strictly ornamental, but in earlier days this was

Our first look at the Pontcysyllte Aqueduct.

indeed where large items were stored.

We also noticed a whole family on the roof of their boat scrubbing with soap and brushes. It was amusing to notice what people store on their stern areas and roofs now; we saw everything from dog crates to bicycles, playpens and motorcycles.

Pets are important on the canals. There seemed to be a definite canal dog prototype, best described as mostly black-and-white border collie but thinner and more rangy looking. It was amazing to us to see how many of the boats sported dogs, and at least 70% of the dogs looked exactly like this type.

One boat, with which we crossed wakes several times, had a dog like this who had a rubber dumbbell on a ribbon pinned to his collar like a child's pacifier. This guy would carry the dumbbell part of the time and the rest of the time he would let it bounce along his chest. He liked to run, and most of the time he jogged along the path and kept pace with his boat.

I wondered how many times his people had had to fish that toy out of the canal before they fastened it to his collar.

We tied up this night in Hindford and ate at a lovely pub called simply *The Narrowboat*.

Bright sun greeted us, and it was my turn to navigate the locks. According to the chart, we had only two more locks to go and then there were none for 20 miles.

The scenery was different again; we spotted rolling hills and pastures and just up ahead we knew we should soon pass into Wales. We stopped for perishables and to frequent a pub that advertised itself as "The Last Pub in England."

Chirk

Through the trees, we got our first glimpse of the Chirk Aqueduct, the first of the two we would cross and our official entry into Wales. Chirk Castle was nearby, an interesting 2-hour diversion for those who have not seen enough English castles.

Chirk Aqueduct, which was begun in 1796 to provide canal access to the coal and limestone deposits of the north, opened in 1801 at a cost of over £20,000. Built as an iron trough it traverses 10 masonry arches, but it was no match for the even more dramatic Pontcysyllte Aqueduct that awaited us later in the day.

Boats could not navigate north of the aqueduct until the 459-foot Chirk Tunnel was completed; this involved mining through solid rock.

Chirk spans the Ceiriog Valley, now a sports playing field. The railway bridge, which came some 40 years later, does not mar the impression. The aqueduct is one-way to the first boat in. My husband, Myron, steered us through in a high wind, and we all had thoughts about the higher and less-protected one yet to come. I wisely decided not to tell anyone about Myron's aversion to heights.

Pushing on

Leaving the aqueduct required a sharp left turn, and we gave the bank a pretty hard smack. This greatly amused two older gentlemen, with their requisite canal dog, who were parked on a bench right at the point where the canal turned. I think they lived for the crunches and we did not disappoint. This was Trevor, the site of another Anglowelsh base. We took advantage of our free septic pump-out here.

As we continued on, suddenly the motor noise of the boat stopped. Up came the floorboards and out came the manual. Somehow, reverse gear had ceased to exist. We were able to continue, but the thought of the lurking Pontcysyllte ahead was pressing. There was no backing out now, or backing up either until we got that motor fixed. Thank goodness, our in-house mechanics got it back fully operational with only a slight delay.

White-knuckle crossing

The Pontcysyllte Aqueduct stretches 127 feet above the raging waters of the River Ed. It is amazing that this feat of engineering is not better known. Pronounced "Pont-ker-sulth-tee," it is over 1,000 feet long and is an iron trough supported by 19 piers. The aqueduct was completed the year of Lord Nelson's death at Trafalgar, 1805, at a cost of £47,018.

No picture can prepare you for that first sight of the aqueduct and the realization that you are going to cross it. . . in a high wind.

Unlike Chirk, it has a severe drop-off just over the trough that gave our boat only a couple inches of leeway. The wind was a gale now, and the boat in front of us, a mere 40 footer, was being blown against the bumper and could make no progress.

Ray jumped out and helped push the boat off the sides of the trough so it could move forward. We were warned by a sign advising us to keep "children and pets under rigorous control."

Myron was still driving, and I could see his terror as he looked down at the valley floor and cascading river.

Obviously, draft animals could never have negotiated this trestle, and we read that they instead were led down the steep banks and across the river while men pulled the boat across the aqueduct. There is a walkway along the trough, but all of us opted to stay in the boat because walking seemed more hazardous.

I personally think we were steered across by a man with his eyes shut tightly, but, in any event, we made it safely. We managed to pry Myron's fingers off the tiller and the next shift took over.

Canal vistas

Across the aqueduct began the beauty of the Vale of Llangollen. Buttresses of limestone cliffs and the purple hue of heather on the hills greeted us. Massive trees, long dead, clung dramatically to the banks and sent up wispy arms against the darkening sky.

This section of the canal, from Trevor to Llangollen, has a history of serious breaches. In 1945 the banks collapsed and swept away the railway; a train fell, killing the driver. But repairs have been made and unless you are watching for Bridge No. 41, you will not recognize the spot.

The canal narrows appreciably here and, except for occasional "turn out" places, traffic becomes one-way. We were fortunate that on this late afternoon we met no other boats on this whole stretch. The towpath was so inviting that several of us chose to walk it and keep pace with the boat.

Llangollen

Soon the rooftops of Llangollen came into view, as well as the old wharf where warehouses have been refurbished as a canal center and museum. We entered the "winding hole" that was the turnaround spot that marked the end of the navigable canal. The wind was fierce and it was necessary to use the long grappling hook to keep us in the deeper water.

We wanted to be turned around and headed outward when we moored for the night. There were many boats already tied up, but we found a good spot near a pleasant bathroom facility. We would occasionally see these nice shower buildings placed there for the use of the boaters.

Suddenly, out of one of the buildings ambled a huge draft horse, completely at liberty. He deliberately walked along the canal and then made a turn down a steep paved road.

Behind him appeared his custodian, also not in any hurry, and we realized that this was the horse who transports tourists in the horse-drawn canal boat the last mile that is not accessible for motorized boats. Visitors ride this boat to see the headwaters of the River Dee at Horseshoe Falls.

Our chart book had warned us that in the busy summer season, it is wise to moor three miles back at Trevor and walk to Llangollen because of the bottlenecks that occur with one-way traffic. We congratulated ourselves again on planning a September trip!

Also from our reading, we learned that every July, Llangollen takes on a completely different tone when it plays host to the Eisteddfod music festival, a national celebration of Welsh music and dancing. This particular evening, however, the slate-gray town looked quiet and inviting.

The wind was still gusty as we wound our way down the steep road that the horse had taken to town. The horse's corral was down there, and he obviously knew his way home because he was munching dinner as we passed.

We crossed the Bishop Trevor Bridge and stopped to watch the cascading waters of the Dee. The noise was deafening, and while the falls were another mile upwater, there were many rapids here also.

Total immersion

We chose a restaurant called *Caesar's* right on the south end of the bridge and thoroughly enjoyed a meal of roast Welsh lamb and appropriate libations.

On our return to the canal, we decided to try a shortcut when we spotted some stairs that seemed to lead directly up to our boat. Friend Ray set out to do some reconnaissance and he soon waved us up.

I went up first, followed by Ray's wife, Jan, who was carrying our only source of light, a torch (flashlight). As soon as I stepped onto the towpath, Ray cautioned me to turn immediately along the path, but Jan did not hear him and she stepped behind him thinking she would turn the beam of the light on the stairs to aid those coming behind.

The next sounds we heard were a scream and a huge splash. It was obvious someone had fallen into the canal, but we did not know who! Each of us called for his partner, and when we saw the torch light shining through the water, we realized it was Jan. She was able to stand in the canal and two of the men were able to lift her out.

We all were quite frightened until Jan, a remarkably good sport, started laughing. We assessed the damage and found her to be missing one shoe, with one ankle beginning to swell and a very soggy purse containing a cell phone and camera.

We got her back to the narrowboat and gave her a hard time about taking a warm shower out of rotation. Her ankle was painful for a day or two, and the cell phone recovered. Alas, the camera did not.

Backtracking

We filled our water tank early the next day and reassessed Jan's ankle, which was swollen but manageable. It was amusing to see her wet clothes spread all over the decks, but it was also sobering to think how close we had come to a serious accident. The canals are not very deep in most places, but the water is full of mud and diesel fuel and an unexpected dunking is never pleasant.

Somewhat later in the journey, we exited a pub another night to find ourselves again right on the edge of the canal, but this time it was at a lock, and the water level was some 20 feet below us. A fall there would have been very serious.

So we learned from our experience to always carry at least one flashlight per couple and to beware of edges and towlines tied *across* the path as we found one night.

We wanted to depart Llangollen before any upstream traffic arrived, so Myron walked the three miles back to Trevor on the towpath and signaled us on the extremely narrow parts. The wind had dissipated and the filtered sunlight made for a most pleasant return through the vale.

I chose to walk across the Pontcysyllte Aqueduct this time to check for any oncoming boats.

As I waited for our boat to make the crossing, I struck up a conversation with a couple from New Zealand who had recently bought a boat and planned to use it for two years on the British waterways. They had family somewhere in Britain and their thought was to stay on the water as long as possible and "go to ground" only during December and January. I admired their fortitude.

We made a return visit to "The Last Pub in England," only in this case it was the first. We passed many boats we now recognized from earlier moorings. Once again we laughed at the canal dog with his tied-on pacifier. We had seen all this scenery before, but because we were going through at a different time of day it all seemed new.

We moored for the evening at *Jack Mytton's Inn and Pub* and, once again, down came the rains. Jack described himself as a "home counties" man, and we would add "with an attitude," but the food was wonderful.

Leisurely day

Our sixth day began with bright sun, but it was much colder. We skipped breakfast in order to get an early start since we needed to be back within an hour of home base by the next night. We stopped for an early lunch at a pub named *Waggoners*, which advertised by a welcoming sign along the canal. The pub was about a quarter mile from the canal, and we enjoyed stretching our legs.

The ivy on the sides of the homes and the pub itself was beginning to turn a brilliant dark red, and we all, except for soggy Jan, got out our cameras.

Later in the afternoon we finished up our snacks, as we were beginning to let our supplies run down. At Willey Moor Locks we got down the stair-steps in record time and stopped at the inn, where the resident cat greeted us.

On the menu for dessert, here in the middle of England, was "Tennessee Grasshopper Pie." (It was awful.) We finished up our Trivial Pursuit championship, where the only Americans reigned supreme.

Wrenbury lock — and all that jazz

Starting out on Thursday, we found ourselves in a part of the canal somewhat narrowed by overgrown vegetation.

At a couple of the locks we got a good look at how the water supply works. Weirs beside the locks release rampages of water that rush at full speed and create a current that must be reckoned with.

By lunchtime we were back at Wrenbury, and this time we got to use our special lock key that activated the bells and whistles and stopped road and bridge traffic.

We spent a little time watching two women painting designs on their boat. We did not ask if they were artists or the boat owners.

We also enjoyed watching a group of schoolchildren who were having a tour of the locks.

We chose the pub right at canalside, called *The Dusty Miller*. Outside was a ring in the side of the brick with a sign stating "Dog Mooring." I had much better luck with the "Tex-Mex Pizza" than I had with the Tennessee offering the night before. In the pub, we recognized accents from America,

Canada, Scotland and South Africa.

We chugged on down the canal, now in shirtsleeves and warm sunshine. At dusk, we arrived again at the **Barbridge Inn** and found a mooring across the canal from the pub; a bridge was conveniently provided for foot traffic, however.

That night at the pub, jazz sounds from the Salt City Jazzmen added to the festivities. It was our last night, so we celebrated and stayed out much later than usual. I fell into my bunk I was so tired, but then I fell into it every night since it was a mere three inches off the floor!

Wrapping up

We were only 1½ hours from the base at Bunbury where it had all begun. We finished packing up and gave the boat a good cleaning. We had realized that suitcases were out of place with such restricted space, so we had all brought soft, crushable bags. This was tricky for us, because we flew from the U.S. with hard-sided bags and then transferred everything for the boat into small bags.

We purchased a mug for Jan — that one we had seen before that stated "I did not fall into the Llangollen Canal!" and Xed out the "not."

We all felt the need for a long, hot shower and comfortable beds, but the experience was unforgettable and not one moment regretted (except by Jan, perhaps).

We agreed that we would "give it another go," as our British friends say. We thought the advantage of going in the off season was great, the lack of crowds balanced by questionable weather. As our friends reminded us, weather in the U.K. is *always* questionable.

We left with the sense that we had seen a part of England and Wales that was virtually unchanged and came away with a feeling of appreciation for a slower, more reflective way of life.

Planning the adventure

For further information, access *narrowboat* on the Internet, or any of the following commercial companies: Alvechurch, Anglowelsh or Black Prince.

The mailing address for Anglowelsh is Anglowelsh Waterway Holidays, 5 Pritchard St., Bristol BS2 8RH, England. Their e-mail address is *AWGP@aol.com*.

Cost varies according to the accommodations required; we paid approximately $750 per couple. This includes free car parking at the base, fuel, septic pump-out and transfer for one-way trips. Major credit cards are accepted and overseas visitors are catered to. (Give Anglowelsh a grocery list and they will stock the boat for you ahead of time at no charge other than for the groceries.)

Also factor in food — reasonable if you eat some meals on board, plus pub rates are very good — and the cost to get to Britain. Off season prices are less costly than summer rates. Make plans a good six to nine months ahead.

The Solway, *our home for the week.*

Scotland

The cannon at Edinburgh Castle announces the beginning of the New Year.

What a way to welcome the New Year — Edinburgh's Hogmanay Festival

HARRYETTE HELSEL, Scarsdale, NY

If you want to participate in an unusual New Year's event, then the place to go is Edinburgh, Scotland.

The buildup

The Hogmanay Festival has been an annual occurrence since the late 1500s. When I attended, the festivities began on the 29th of December with a torchlight procession consisting of adults, children, bands and street performers starting at Parliament Square in the center of the city and proceeding down the main Princes Street and continuing one mile to Calton Hill.

Preceding page: Bagpiper in Edinburgh. — Photo by Theodore Lewis

---

Thousands of people had purchased torches, donating the money to charity; this time the money collected went to Scottish European Aid and the local children and land-mine victims of Bosnia.

Seeing the multitude of torches winding their way around the town in an orderly fashion was quite a sight to behold. The walk culminated in a fireworks display from the hilltop.

Along Princes Street several blocks had been cordoned off for a winter fairground with game booths and various rides. There was fun for young and old.

From Dec. 30 to Jan. 1 different events took place throughout the city. Most were free.

Some excellent concerts were held in the cathedral, the newly refurbished Festival Theatre and the castle.

Stages were erected in various areas of the city and different bands performed. Among them were jazz, Celtic, Scottish, Latin and Cajun. Huge MTV monitors were situated along the streets near the stages.

Movie matinees for children were available as well as a "Magic Mirror Tent" where Scotland's favorite magician, Magic Bob, entertained. Other performers were Mr. Boom, Green Ginger and The Happy Gang, a singalong group.

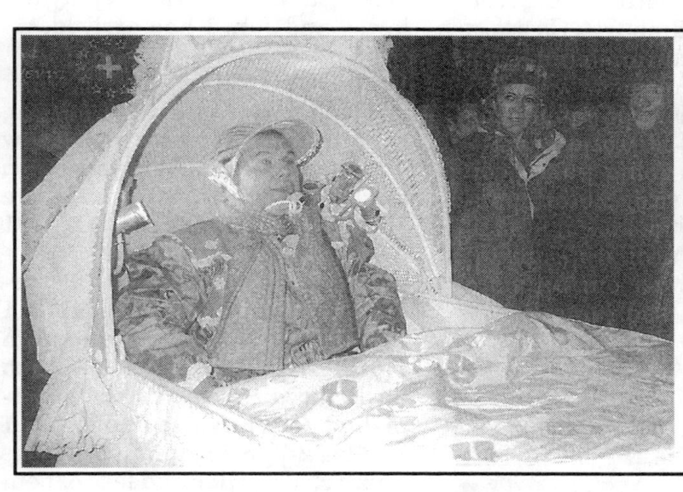

Street performer in a motorized baby carriage.

The main event

Dec. 31 finally arrived. Three major thoroughfares were cordoned off for about a square mile. Only people wearing wristbands were allowed into the area. Visitors could receive wristbands from the hotel at which they were staying or from the Hogmanay Events Office.

A map revealed authorized entrance and exit areas; designated policemen and emergency medical help were located throughout the streets. The crowd appeared to be quite orderly.

The big street fair began around 10 p.m.

Some of the unusual street performers included Les Big Brozeurs (from Lyon). Four bespectacled men dressed in beige trench coats towering about 10 feet above the crowd kept mingling with people and established an atmosphere of fun as they moved their elongated necks up and down playing the role of clowns.

A man dressed as a baby sat in a motorized baby carriage weaving in and out of the crowd. A stage was set up to create weird hairdos for anyone who was brave enough to partake in a makeover.

As the minutes passed, the crowds seemed to enlarge. By midnight 200,000 people had gathered in the area. Suddenly the roar of

Street fairground.

a cannon was heard coming from the beautiful Edinburgh Castle on the hill — signifying midnight. A spectacular fireworks display followed and Jan. 1 had arrived.

Les Big Brozeurs from Lyon were among the street performers.

To participate

If you are interested in doing something different next New Year's, you can book your own flight and hotel and call the Hogmanay Box Office (011 0131 473 1998) for a schedule.

You can plan your stay at top-of-the-line **Hotel Balmoral** (011 0131 556 2414) or **Caledonian Hotel** (011 0131 225 2433), both on Princes Street, or the refurbished **Roxburghe Hotel** (011 0131 225 3921) on Charlotte Square, a smaller and less expensive hotel excellently located.

The weather is unpredictable. It could rain, snow or be sunny. Fifty-degree temperature with sporadic sun and rain was the norm during my stay.

Additional diversions

Each day was spent sightseeing

a different area. One day I took the 50-minute train ride to Glasgow and went to various museums, hiring a taxi to tour the city.

Another day I took a bus tour to St. Andrews, the home of the Royal and Ancient Golf Club whose old course is one of the most famous in the world and where golf originated. Along the way I stopped at a fishing village.

Another day was spent touring the Trossachs area, where the terrain is covered with a rust underbrush and is quite pretty to view.

The city of Edinburgh is very historic and has many sights to see, such as the castle, museums, Parliament House and Palace of Holyroodhouse. The Festival Theatre had a wonderful production of "Tosca" produced by the Scottish Opera Company.

Shopping is abundant. At the time of my visit, one pound equaled $1.55 and, to my chagrin, my purchasing power was diminished.

The salmon is excellent and haggis (heart, lungs and liver of a sheep with suet, oatmeal and onion) is interesting to digest and truly Scottish, as are the different malt liquors. There are endless restaurants and pubs from which to choose.

New Year's at Edinburgh was very enjoyable! I experienced one week packed full of wonderful new experiences.

Orkney and Shetland in early summer

MARGARET & ROGER HINKLE, Arvada, CO

We visited the Orkney and Shetland Islands during late June and early July 1997. Our particular interest was in seeing the world-famous Neolithic and Iron Age sites.

"Come across; I'll wait"

Flying from Aberdeen into Kirkwall, the main town of Orkney, we saw several almost treeless but very green islands. To the west was the hilly island of Hoy, while the flat, large island of Mainland is connected by causeways to the smaller islands of Lamb Holm, Glimps Holm, Burray and South Ronaldsay.

We picked up our rental car (£31, or about $51, a day including tax) from Scarth Hire, the agent for National Car Rental, through which we had booked in the U.S., and headed to Stromness on the western side of Mainland. We had reservations there at the **Ferry Inn** (phone +44 [1856] 850-280 or fax +44 [1856] 851-332) for £48 ($79) per night for a double room with bathroom en suite and including a hearty breakfast.

We selected Stromness as a base because of its proximity to the majority of the archaeological sites that we had come to see. Although prehistoric sites were our prime interest, we also saw museums and historical places and learned about the strategic importance of Orkney in World War II.

Stromness and the Ferry Inn were bustling with hiking and diving groups. Divers wore dry suits for cold-water diving, primarily over the ships sunk in Scapa Flow, the strait separating Mainland

Roger Hinkle stands beside the passage door inside of Maes Howe.

from the southern islands. In the evenings, the Ferry Inn pub was filled with happy people drinking beer, eating pub grub and recounting their day's adventures.

Stromness also has the historic **Stromness Hotel**, which was a World War II U.S. military headquarters. The Stromness Hotel is more formal and more expensive than the Ferry Inn, but it appeared to be a very nice place to stay. It also serves a delicious Orkney-fudge cheesecake. Several bed-and-breakfasts are in the area, as well.

The culture on Orkney is generally laid-back, relaxed, friendly and helpful. Drivers are polite: when two cars approach a one-lane bridge, one driver flashes his headlights, not to say "Watch out; I'm coming through first" but to say "Come across; I'll wait for you!"

Weather conditions were cool, with 50s (°F) days and 40s nights. We ran the electric heater in our hotel room every night. Even in summer, a person often needs a wool sweater in addition to a good windbreaker/waterproof jacket, hat and often gloves for outdoor excursions.

Waterproof pants to pull on over your regular pants plus rubber shoes or boots are also needed because the weather can change from sunny to rainy to sunny again in only a few minutes.

Skara Brae Neolithic village

People arrived on Orkney in the Neolithic Age, soon after the glaciers retreated, probably walking across a land bridge from mainland Scotland or arriving in small boats as the sea level rose. These people left Orkney dotted with archaeological sites, most of which can be accessed from the main roads.

Highlights of the Neolithic sites are the Skara Brae village on the

Bay of Skaill, about eight miles north of Stromness, and the Maes Howe tomb along the A965 about halfway between Finstown and Stromness.

Skara Brae (3100-2600 B.C.) is one of the best-preserved prehistoric villages in Europe, primarily because it lay buried and protected by sand dunes until a big storm uncovered it in 1850.

The excavated village consists of six roofless, semisubterranean stone houses and a workshop connected by subterranean passageways that helped protect people from the ever-present wind; the village probably was very comfortable for its time.

Roof-high middens of seashells are evidence of a major food source and show that some of the houses originally may have been above ground level.

The people also raised cattle, sheep and goats and had small fields of grains.

Not only were the house walls constructed of flat stones but the interior furnishings were too, including wall niches, "cupboards," and box bed frames which would have been filled with lichens and skins for sleeping. It seems as though the occupants had only recently moved and left their querns and stone furnishings.

At Skara Brae we purchased one-year season passes for Historic Scotland sites; the cost was about £9 ($15) each for senior citizens (Old-Age Pensioners, or "OAPs," in Britain), a savings of nearly 50% over separate admission tickets to numerous archaeological and historical sites.

Tombs and stone circles

Maes Howe means "high land surrounded by marsh," an excellent description of the hill-shaped tomb standing above flat farmland and visible from miles away. The tomb was constructed of overlapping flagstones and is surrounded by a ditch. You enter stooping through a long, low entry passage into a 15-foot-high central chamber with side burial chambers.

The sturdy, modern-looking interior construction belies the fact that the tomb was built over 4,700 years ago! About 1,000 years ago, Norse tomb-raiders carved graffiti on the interior walls with their axes. A translation of their runic writings is available inside the tomb; many writers left their names plus other graffiti concerning their lady-friends and their searches for buried treasure.

Admission to the tomb is only by joining a guided small group because of the small size of the interior chamber; we used our Historic Scotland passes for admission here.

The stone circles called Stones of Stenness (3000-2500 B.C.) and the Ring of Brodgar (2500-2000 B.C.) are located close to Maes Howe, at the southern end of the strip of land separating the Loch of Harray from the Loch of Stenness. The Stones of Stenness consist of four 15- to 20-foot-tall standing flat stones surrounding two adjacent stones about six feet tall.

The many standing stones of the Ring of Brodgar are slightly shorter than those at Stenness; however, Brodgar seems more impressive because of its large size (about 350 feet in diameter) and surrounding ditch. Both sites are well signposted, unattended and free.

Along the A965, on the south shore of the Loch of Stenness, you can see the small, grass-covered hill above the Unstan Chambered Cairn in a field near a house. The cairn is on private land (no admission charge, however).

Park beside the buildings and walk along a fenced path out to the cairn. You crawl into the flagstone-constructed tomb on your hands and knees, then stand upright beneath a new, skylighted roof to see the burial chambers in the sides of the tomb.

Broch of Gurness

Ruined stone towers called "brochs" abound in Orkney (and also in Shetland). The brochs were built in the Iron Age about 2,000 years ago, both for lookouts and for protection in case of attack. Villages grew up around the brochs, occupied by people in the Iron Age, then Picts and finally Norse, each group utilizing stones from older buildings for their own constructions.

The largest village on Mainland is the Broch of Gurness, near Aikerness on the northeast side of the island; we used our Historic Scotland passes here.

This impressive site was occupied from the first century B.C. until the Viking age; the stone tower originally was nearly 35 feet high. People in this village traded with people in similar villages on the nearby island of Rousay, crossing the Eynhollow Sound by canoe. A fierce wind was blowing the day we visited (apparently, this is a very windy area — one guidebook advises visiting on "calm" days) and we were glad we didn't have to cross the water by canoe.

Brough of Birsay

The Brough of Birsay is a large, Pictish-Norse settlement on Brough Head Island off the northwest tip of Mainland, about a 25-minute drive from Stromness.

The site can be reached only during a few hours each day at low tide by hiking across the causeway separating the island from the mainland; consult the tourist office in Stromness for tidal schedules. Even the curator at the visitors' center has to hike across and sometimes is isolated there when the causeway is flooded!

We used our Historic Scotland passes here also. You enter the brough grounds by hiking up the old Viking boat slip. The most identifiable ruin is of a Norse church. Nearby, Viking long-house foundations were built over Pict house foundations; some Celtic foundations also remain. We were intrigued by the Viking village drainage system emptying over the sea cliff; the stone slabs covering the drain are still in place.

Many groups come to the island to hike along the cliffs.

The 16th-century Earl's Palace at Birsay on the mainland side of the causeway is worth a half hour of wandering through the roofless building complex, imagining what life here must have been like 400 years ago. It was built by the Earl of Orkney, Robert Stewart, in the latter half of the 16th century. The palace grounds are unattended; admission is free.

Liddle Burnt Mound

The Iron Age Liddle Burnt Mound and 5,000-year-old Isbister Chambered Tomb are located about a mile apart on the southeastern shore of the island of

South Ronaldsay, which is accessible by road from Mainland; they are well worth the drive.

Take the A961 south from Kirkwall, Mainland, to Burwick on South Ronaldsay, then the B9041 east and follow the signs.

These highly intriguing sites are on a working farm where the owners are also the site curators (admission is £2.50 per person). The owners have assembled an educational, "hands-on" display of excavated artifacts and bones (including human skulls); they also sell postcards, guidebooks and educational materials.

A young woman family member gave us an enthusiastic and personalized presentation about the excavations and artifacts. As we prepared to hike to the archaeological sites, the skies opened up to a heavy rain. We put on our waterproof jackets and pants but had forgotten our own advice and had left our rubber shoes in the hotel.

"No problem — put on a pair of our Wellingtons," said the young lady as she showed us a couple dozen pairs of waterproof boots in various sizes just for visitors on rainy days.

Wearing the borrowed Wellingtons, we hiked about a mile to the Burnt Mound, adjacent to a marsh with flowing water. The rain abated and we soon were joined by the farm's owner, who arrived on a motorbike.

He explained that "burnt mound" was a term given by early archaeologists to describe stone-slab-lined pits such as this that were filled with fire-blackened stones. The pits were actually cooking pits; they were always located near a source of water so that the pit could be filled with water and heated by tossing in hot stones.

Tomb of the Eagles

After studying the burnt mound site, we hiked another mile to the Isbister Tomb, located near a cliff at the edge of the North Sea. The tomb is popularly known as the Tomb of the Eagles because of the over 300 mummified sea eagles found there; the birds were believed to be clan totems that were placed in the tomb for religious reasons.

As at the Unstan Chambered Cairn, you enter the tomb on your hands and knees (almost on your stomach) through a low passage, then stand up in the center, which is now covered by a skylighted roof.

However, unlike the Unstan cairn, the Tomb of the Eagles contains some of the bones of the people originally interred there. Neolithic people on Orkney exposed their dead to the elements until the flesh was gone, then organized the disarticulated bones in different chambers inside the tomb — skulls in one chamber (you can see six of them behind a glass wall), long bones in another chamber and so forth.

Historic farmhouses

Until the late 1800s, many farmers on Orkney cooked and heated their stone houses using fireplaces. The Corrigall Old Farm Museum on Mainland (£2 per person also includes admission to the nearby Kirbuster Farm Museum) is well signposted, just east of the A986 road and about halfway between its junctions with A965 and B9057.

Fish drying over a peat fire in a kitchen at the Corrigall Old Farm Muesum. Note the Orkney chair.

It illustrates the comfort level of farmers' lives only 100 years ago. When we visited, fish were drying over a smoky peat fire in the kitchen fireplace.

The occupants of the home could sit and warm themselves in front of the fireplace in their "Orkney chairs" — straight, high-backed chairs with curved sides to protect a person from drafts. The Orkney chairs either had wooden backs or backs woven of thick straw rope; some chairs had built-in bottom drawers for storage.

Woodworking shops in Kirkwall build various styles of these chairs now and ship them to people who want one for their own home. The curiously attractive, full-sized chairs sell for several hundred pounds, but 4- to 5-inch-high models sell for £20 to £35 ($33-$58).

Kirkwall sights

Kirkwall, the main city on Orkney, is an attractive, quiet town with several shops. The Tankerness House Museum has artifacts from Neolithic to medieval times.

Our Scottish Heritage Pass admitted us here also. Saint Magnus Cathedral (constructed in the 12th to 15th centuries) has many 16th- to 17th-century tombstones with carved skulls and bones. Evidently, the people buried in the church were very concerned with propriety; several tombstones bear engravings such as, "Here lyes an honest man (man's name), his discreet wife (woman's name), and their lawful son/daughter (child's name)."

Orkney in World War II

The interisland causeways that we saw while flying into Kirkwall were originally constructed during World War II as the Churchill Barriers to prevent German submarine movement into the Scapa Flow. Because Scapa Flow is a natural shelter from the North Atlantic, over the centuries many ships have been anchored and sunk here; these ships now attract divers. The largest number of ships were sunk during battles in World War I.

In 1940, at the beginning of World War II, the British attempted to prevent further ship loss by building the Churchill Barriers out of scuttled ships, rocks and other debris; you can see the scuttled ships as you drive across the causeways.

Some of the workers building the barriers were Italian prisoners of war. A group of these prisoners built the "Italian Chapel" on Lamb Holm. The church was constructed from two domed, metallic, military Quonset-type huts, which are not immediately apparent when you look at the false-front facade of the chapel. The interior walls were so artistically painted that you have to touch them to realize they are not real stone and tile.

One afternoon we took the ferry from Stromness to North Hoy (£2.20 per person, round trip), with a stop at Graemsay. Seeing the large, sunken block-ship in the sound between Graemsay and Hoy and the prominent gun emplacements and bunkers guarding Hoy Sound along the north coast of the island made us realize the strategic importance of Orkney during World War II.

Orkney overview

Our visit to Orkney impressed us with the fact that these seemingly remote islands have been important crossroads of humanity for thousands of years. We had seen many remarkable sights, but many more remained to be seen. We'll return someday to Orkney.

Shetland

Our flight from Kirkwall, Orkney, to the Shetland airport at Sumburgh took 40 minutes. From the air, Shetland looks as green as Orkney but is much more hilly, with a few stands of trees on sheltered hillsides. North of Lerwick the scenery is especially beautiful, with high peat and heather moors separated by deep, water-filled valleys called "voes."

At the airport we picked up our rental car (£32, or near $53, a day including tax) from Bolts Car Hire, the agent for National Car Rental, which we had booked in the U.S., and headed north to the main town of Lerwick.

We stayed at the **Queen's Hotel** in Lerwick [phone +44 (1595) 692-826 or fax +44 (1595) 694-048] for £74 ($122) per night for a double room with en suite bathroom and including full breakfast. Our room had a good view of the waterfront and of the reproduction Viking ship that takes tourists around the harbor when it's not too windy.

Temperatures on Shetland were similar to those on Orkney, but the wind was much stronger, reaching "gale force 8" on July 1st. Several shops in Lerwick sell Shetland wool sweaters, a necessity for us every day because of the windchill.

Located opposite Bergen, Norway, at about 60 degrees north latitude, Shetland actively supported the Norwegian resistance during World War II by transporting men and arms across the sea at night. Many Norwegians were

Overview of wheelhouse and Norse foundations — Jarlshof.

visiting Shetland while we were there.

The people on Shetland are just as friendly and helpful as those on Orkney, but their cultures are different. The presence of North Sea oil money is obvious on Shetland, with many new housing developments, wide new roads and an "all-business" atmosphere.

Prehistoric sites

Mainland Shetland has four prehistoric sites worthy of more than casual attention. We visited the Jarlshof site near the airport at Sumburgh, the Clickimin Broch at Lerwick and the Stanydale "temple" in north Shetland. The high winds kept boats from taking us to the Broch of Mousa on Mousa Island south of Lerwick.

Located just south of the airport grounds, Jarlshof is the most important archaeological site in Shetland; we used our Historic Scotland passes here. Jarlshof is a large, multilayered site ranging in age from prehistoric to 17th century.

At least three hours can be spent hiking around the several acres of ruins, crawling through underground Iron Age storage chambers and investigating a Pictish "wheelhouse," or circular stone house with radial stone piers that both supported a thatch roof and divided the house into sections for different purposes. Climb the stairs to the viewpoint atop the ruins of the 17th-century "laird's castle" for the best overview of the whole site.

Each group of occupants utilized building materials from previous occupants for construction, making Jarlshof an intriguing but very complicated place to understand; one definitely needs a guidebook.

Both the **Jarlshof Hotel** restaurant and pub on the opposite side of the Jarlshof ruins car park serve very tasty lunches to fortify you for your exertions here.

The prehistoric and Iron Age Clickimin Broch is easily seen, as it is in a large field on the south side of Lerwick, across the road from a housing development.

The broch originally sat on a small island in the freshwater Clickimin Loch, but the loch has been mostly drained and it's now a marshy area adjacent to the broch. Inside the stone broch you can see two or three levels of floors and passages. The site is unattended and admission is free.

The 5,000-year-old Stanydale "temple" is located south of the A971 between Lerwick and Walls, far from any town. About two miles west of Bixter, follow a signposted minor road about two miles south to the Stanydale trailhead; park and walk across the fields for about three-quarters of a mile to the partly excavated site.

The partially restored building foundation is believed to have been a Neolithic tribal assembly hall, unique for its large size. The desolate location of the Stanydale site gives it a mysterious atmosphere that probably led to its early designation as a temple.

The Catpund steatite quarries near Cunningsburgh are worth a stop. Located about halfway between Lerwick and Sumburgh, they can be accessed from a car park along the west side of the A970 at Catpund Burn.

From prehistoric until medieval times people made bowls from the steatite (soapstone) rock lining the gully; you can see the carved-out places where stone blanks were removed from the rock walls for later hollowing-out and finishing.

We had read that the best stone excavations can be seen near the head of the gully, but we were discouraged from hiking that far by the "Beware of Rams" sign at the car park.

Boat-roofed shed at Shetland Croft Museum — Voe, Mainland.

Other sights on Mainland

The Shetland Croft Museum is worth a visit; it is signposted east of the A970 at Southvoe, about four miles north of the Sumburgh airport (admission £1.50). Situated in a beautiful location near the sea, the museum illustrates the difficult life of Shetland farmers 100 years ago.

The stone house and farm buildings are similar to those at the farm museums on Orkney. Interesting outbuildings include a thatch-roofed stone mill near a creek and a stone shed that utilized a worn-out boat for a roof.

The restored Quendale Mill is a large, imposing building located about three miles north of the Sumburgh airport and about two miles west of the A970. Water from the adjacent creek turned a waterwheel which turned the stones used to grind various grains. The admission fee of £1 included a guided tour with a very detailed explanation of the operation of the mill. There was also a nice little gift shop with some locally made craft work for sale.

Driving north from Lerwick we saw large, open areas of peat and heather and many beautiful views of voes and the sea.

Near Brae we crossed over Mavis Grind, a narrow strip of land that separates the Atlantic Ocean from the North Sea. Many prehistoric cairns lie in the Mavis Grind area, but most of them are so poorly preserved that they are nearly indistinguishable from generic piles of rocks.

At Sullom Voe, along the B9076, we looked at the large North Sea oil terminal which is a main source of income for the modern facilities on Shetland.

The old (1900) **St. Magnus Hotel** at the community of Hillswick, along the A970 on the west side of Ura Firth, is said to be the only hotel on Shetland constructed entirely of wood; all the wood was shipped from Norway. We stopped here for delicious pie and coffee.

Shetland overview

We were very glad we chose to visit Shetland. The combination of wide, green landscape surrounded by blue sea, along with the wind and cool, fresh air, has a seemingly contradictory effect of both tranquilizing and stimulating a person. We saw only the main island; the other islands hold sights yet to be seen.

This Italian Chapel at Lamb Holm, Orkney was built by Italian POWs during construction of Churchill Barriers during WWII.

Orkney Isles: Italian Chapel

Scotland's Orkney Isles are well know to archaeologists for their Stone Age settlements, especially Skara Brae, one of Europe's best preserved, dating back some 5,000 years. But a more recent bit of history deserves a visit: the lovely Italian Chapel, built by Italian POWs inside two Nissen huts in WWII. It's located just beyond the first of the Churchill Barriers which were constructed to connect the lesser islands to the mainland.

– *JAN ROUTLEY, Durham, NH*

Wales

Photo by Katharine McCormack

Aberystwyth, Wales. Notice the signposts: after crossing into Wales from England, all directional signs are in both Welsh and English.

B&B auto tour of enchanting Wales

EMILEE HINES, Portsmouth, VA

When Margaret Lloyd visited us in Virginia, she said, "Now, you must let me show you Wales." She made the perfect guide — easygoing and adventurous, she'd grown up in Wales and still remembered Welsh.

Although all the British Isles are well served by trains and public coaches, the ideal way to travel is by car, with a Britsh driver who's been there.

Traveling British-style

We set off westward on A40 from her home in Cheltenham on a dark, rainy morning. However, by the time we stopped for mid-morning tea, the slashing rain had lightened to a fine mist; by noon it had stopped altogether.

Even in the gloom, Wales is enchanting.

At the first ruined castle I spotted, I cried, "Stop! Let me get a picture."

She didn't even slow down: "You'll see hundreds of castles, including Caernarfon, where Charles was made Prince of Wales. And we'll have better weather, I'm confident."

We traveled in typical British fashion, carrying in the "boot" of her car a large thermos of hot tea, a hamper of fresh fruit, sandwiches, individual meat pies from Marks and Spencer, packages of tea biscuits and sweets plus cutlery, cups and a blanket for picnics.

We ate lunch below the ruins of Llansteffan Castle, overlooking a peaceful bay.

"Dylan Thomas wrote of visiting here a number of times as a child, coming by boat or dog cart," Margaret said. "Unfortunately, we don't have a boat."

Thomas museum

Getting to Laugharne, almost considered a shrine by Dylan Thomas fans, took us past ancient farms on narrow, hedge-bordered roads (Rte. A4066).

The town itself is easy to get around in and is well marked. We parked at a municipal lot beside Laugharne Castle and Bay and walked uphill past shops and the white-stucco town hall to a dramatic promontory overlooking the water, then continued down a series of steps to Thomas' boathouse.

A brilliant tangle of garden surrounds the boathouse, now a museum of Thomas memorabilia. After browsing, visitors can linger for lunch or tea on the veranda.

Back at the parking lot, a "boot sale" was in progress — a rummage sale from the trunks of cars.

By then the sun was out and the sky was a clear blue. A walk from another parking lot took us to Thomas' grave in the middle of the church cemetery — a simple cross marked with his name and the dates.

On to St. David's

We went back on A487 to Haverfordwest, then to the village of Spittal, where Margaret grew up. We visited the 2-room rock schoolhouse she had attended (now a museum) and the quaint stone church where her mother is buried on a gentle green hillside.

Our destination that night was St. David's, on the westernmost point of south Wales.

Tradition has it that David, the patron saint of Wales, was born and buried there. He established a monastery that, being close to the sea, was ravaged, burned or destroyed 13 times between 645 and 1097.

The present cathedral and adjacent ruins, dating from the 12th century, are eloquent reminders of religious life in a troubled time — storage rooms, fish ponds, gatehouse and parapets.

We walked among the haunting stonework in the lengthening twilight as "A Midsummer Night's Dream" was being presented. We visited again the following morning.

Not so accommodating

We stayed at **Ramsay House**, which had excellent food but less than pleasant accommodations, due chiefly to the owner's attitude.

Our room was so tiny, we could barely walk between the two beds, and the shower in the bathroom across the hall was inoperable.

As after-dinner coffee was served, the owner walked around with a bottle of brandy, offering, "a few drops in your coffee to give you a restful Welsh evening." When we checked out, we discovered that his offer of "a few drops" had cost us each $3!

Breakfast was at 8:30 and checkout time was an incredibly early 9:00—and he would not allow us to leave the car even a few minutes extra to walk three blocks to the drugstore and return.

Following the coast

We followed the coast northward to Fishguard, home of Margaret's father's family and the site where "Under Milk Wood" was filmed.

We walked among the circular Gorsedd Rocks, a smaller version of Stonehenge.

From these stones the land drops down precipitously to the sea. . . to pounding waves in one direction and a protected harbor in another.

All afternoon we followed the coast road, catching glimpses of the sea as we passed rolling green fields grazed by cattle and flocks of sheep. Wales is varying shades of peaceful green dotted with creamy white and brown.

Recommended B&B

We ate supper at *Dylanwad dwa*, an excellent restaurant in Dolgellau (pronounced Dol-geth-luh), and found our way to **Ystumgwern Hall Farm** for the night. (This B&B has been recommended by other ***ITN*** readers for its cleanliness and its owners, John and Jane Williams, for their friendliness. Write Ystumgwern Hall Farm, Dyffryn Arduwy, Gwynedd LL 44 2DD, Wales, U.K.; phone 0341-247-249.)

We had allotted £20 per person per night for accommodations and stayed within our budget throughout the trip.

We fell asleep in our comfortable room under the eaves, with its own tiny, immaculate bathroom, hearing the nostalgic sound of a train nearby.

When we came down to breakfast the next morning, Jane Williams had just finished scrubbing the back steps leading out to the farm with hot, sudsy water.

She prepared a sumptuous breakfast of farm-fresh eggs, bacon and milk plus cereal, fruit and Welsh fried bread to send us on our way.

"Great Little Trains"

We followed A496 past Harlech Castle on across a tiny toll bridge to Porthmadog, terminal of the Ffestiniog Railroad.

Railroad buffs should plan ahead to include a ride on one of the many "Great Little Trains of Wales," as the brochure calls them. Most are narrow gauge and operate only in spring and summer.

Ffestiniog, one of the most scenic, leaves Porthmadog for Blaenau Ffestiniog — a historic slate-mining town — five times a day in summer. Change there for the main line to Betws-y-Coed, Llandudno and Manchester. Or, return to Porthmadog after having tea.

The other "Great Little Trains" are located throughout Wales. A single Wanderer Ticket makes it possible to ride all eight trains any eight days out of 15 for about $50 for adults or $25 for children.

Tickets and brochures are available from GLTW, Pant Station, Dowlais, Merthyr Tydfil, Mid Glamorgan CF48 2UP, Wales, U.K, or at the stations of any of the railroads.

Portmeirion

At Porthmadog we toured Portmeirion, a wealthy man's recreation of a bit of Italy in Wales.

Pastel-pretty and lush with flowers and greenery, it offers a few hours of pleasant strolling—but it isn't really Italian, and it isn't in keeping with Wales.

It has clean rest rooms, lodging available for the night, and lovely views of the beach. It's a favorite of honeymooners. Next time, I'll skip it and see more truly Welsh sights.

Mount Snowdon

We turned inland through the

Caernarfon Castle where the Prince of Wales is invested.

wooded, mountainous Snowdonia National Park.

At Beddgelert (named for the dog that mistakenly was thought to have killed a child and was tragically put to death in a famous Welsh story) we passed the Sygun Copper Mine.

This attraction, which recreates the Victorian heydey of copper mining, has received the Prince of Wales Award for tourism.

On our sunny Saturday, Mount Snowdon was thick with hikers, and the frequent rack-and-pinion trains to the summit were all booked. We saw the nearby slate quarry and drove on to Caernarfon Castle, one of the "must see" castles in Britain.

Mighty Caernarfon

Caernarfon has everything: towers, turrets, parapets, gun slits, a mighty King's Gate and a tidal moat with a drawbridge.

Begun in 1283, this is no livable castle with paintings and draperies but a fortress, powerful and austere.

In this century Caernarfon was the site of the investiture of Charles, Prince of Wales, and of EdwardVIII, who was briefly king.

Within the towers are four museums. I found the Royal Welch Fusiliers Regimental Museum and the dramatic film of Welsh history in the Eagle Tower most interesting.

However, unless I missed seeing an elevator hidden somewhere, the only way to the Eagle Tower is a steep, winding stairway. Margaret at 5'1" could barely reach from step to step.

It's a pity the access is so difficult, for the audiovisual program is superb, pulling together the threads of English-Welsh conflict as well as the history of the castle itself.

In our search for the perfect vantage point for a photo of

Caernarfon, we were caught for a time on the wrong side of the drawbridge when it lifted. It was a good lesson on how drawbridges protected castles.

B&B find

We stayed that night at the best B&B of our trip, **Caer Siddi**, a former Georgian vicarage four miles east of Caernarfon.

From our spacious, high-ceilinged room we had a lovely view of Mount Snowdon and a silvery stretch of water. We had time for a walk in the walled garden before an elegant seafood dinner, and afterward joined four other guests by the fire in the parlor for tea.

The owner, Audrey Pierce, was a superb hostess. In addition to preparing excellent meals, she went out of her way to be helpful.

When we came down to breakfast the next morning, she was on the phone trying to arrange passage to Ireland for some guests who had decided at the last minute to go.

Caer Siddi is at Llanddeiniolen, Caernarfon, Gwynedd LL55 3AD, Wales, U.K.; phone 248-670-462.

Betws-y-Coed

To avoid duplicating our previous day's route, we went northeast on B4366 to join A5, the major road to Betws-y-Coed. (The "Coed" is not pronounced like our word for college student but as if it were "cawid.")

This picturesque little town is on my list for a longer stay next time. Three rivers join there to flow beneath a historic stone bridge.

There are a railway museum and a museum of vintage cars (Motor Museum), and the town is the gateway to Snowdonia National Park.

Horseshoe Pass

Route A5 would have taken us to Llangollen, but we turned northeastward on A5104 and then southward on A542 to drive the famous Horseshoe Pass. This wild, scenic route was beautiful even in the morning mist.

Flocks of sheep have the right of way but are so used to people that they approach for handouts and photo opportunities at the scenic overlooks.

We came into Llangollen from the north, past Valle Crucis Abbey.

Llangollen

Llangollen was hosting a Victorian festival and a display of antique trains, so the town was teeming with visitors.

We parked in one of the outlying car parks and took the footpath down to the town, crossing the stone bridge across the River Dee. Crowds on the bridge were eagerly pointing down to the tumbling water, saying they'd just seen salmon.

After mid-morning coffee by the fireplace in the lounge of the Riverbend Hotel, we shopped for pottery and woolen fabric (both made nearby) in the crowded shops and looked at the railway display.

We saved the main attraction, the horse-drawn boat trips, for last. Gliding along the canal on one of these boats is a trip into the past, or into the world of "Wind in the Willows." There is no harsh motor, only the clip-clop of a horse's hooves.

While waiting for our turn on

the boat, we looked at the horses and the small Canal Museum. Boat trips are available daily from Easter to September.

I had imagined a bountiful Sunday dinner at some paneled dining room, but we discovered to our dismay that the restaurants in small towns close for Sunday dinner. We ate the remains of our provisions from the boot of the car, standing in a deserted store parking lot.

Winding back to Cheltenham We arrived early at **Corven Hall**, our Bed & Breakfast just outside the Victorian spa town, Llandrindod Wells.

There still are places there where one can "take the waters," and the town, with its elaborate houses and hotels, is worth seeing.

Corven Hall is popular with families, perhaps because of its large rooms and rural setting, and the food was good and typically Welsh.

We returned to Cheltenham by way of Radnor Forest, crossing Offa's Dyke. Earthen remains are still visible of the ancient wall built as a line of demarcation between England and Wales.

We had lunch at Ludlow, which has its own castle right in town and narrow, crooked streets winding past half-timbered buildings.

After seeing Ludlow Castle and shopping in the fruit and vegetable markets, we drove to Hereford for the very interesting Cider Museum.

There I discovered perry, which is a cider-like drink made from pears, not apples. We bought a bottle, as well as several bottles of apple brandy, and back home celebrated a safe and scenic trip.

Excellent guidebooks on Wales as well as "Wales Bed and Breakfast" are available for about $5 from the British Tourist Authority, 551 Fifth Ave., Ste.701, New York, NY 10176-0799.

I'm already planning a further trip to Wales.

Curious sheep approach travelers at Horseshoe Pass.

Full of fussy turrets, cupolas, etc., is the famous spa touwn of Llandrindod Wells. — Photos by Phyllis Gavitt Harris

Touring Wales by rental car

ARTHUR S. HARRIS, Jr., Arlington, VT

Manual transmission cars are still a majority in Europe, so it seemed sensible that, in reserving a car for a tour of Wales, we reject an expensive automatic for a stick-shift VW Golf. Why not? Phyllis and I grew up on such cars.

Yes, we anticipated that shifting with the left hand would be a minor adjustment, as would be driving for 12 days on the left side of the road at which we had limited experience.

We were, however, unprepared for the roads and occasional highways of Wales. Also road signage. Not just the fact that all signs were bilingual (Welsh and English), but we never saw North, South, East or West indicators — common all over the USA — when intersecting a numbered highway.

Where are the shoulders?

We felt our adjustment to Welsh roads would go easily because we live in Vermont, a state with more gravel than dirt roads and dominated by 2-lane blacktop roads with a stripe down the middle. Often, there's no passing for miles on our serpentine roads.

But at least our roads have shoulders. If a big logging truck is headed our way, a simple light hand on the steering wheel pulls us partly over onto the shoulder. We give such trucks a wide berth. This is not so easily done in Wales.

After picking up our rental car in Cardiff ("Europe's newest capital"), we soon realized that most rural roads were shoulderless. We couldn't pull over too much to the left without the risk of scraping the side of the VW with hedgerows or, worse, 2-foot-high slate stone walls hugging the edge of the pavement.

So, instead of careening around the country (about the size of Massachusetts) at near the official speed limit (60 mph on single "carriageways," 70 on "dual carriageways and motorways"), we drove defensively.

Rounding a bend, we were ever alert for a road-hogging lorry or a herd of sheep crossing the road ahead.

Consequently, all suggested driving times in various guidebooks and pamphlets were way off. They seemed to exist for experienced locals who were familiar with every curve and roundabout.

Adding to our slow times was our feeling that we should get out of the way of tailgating cars, so we were forever pulling into side-of-the-road bus stops or "pull-offs" to let locals whiz past.

Pleasant populace

Never once did anyone honk behind us, or flick high beams, or give us a gesture in passing. And when once or twice we stalled in a village and took a moment to restart the engine, there was nary an impatient horn toot.

We're suspicious of travel accounts which proclaim, "The people of (fill in the blank) are friendly."

But the Welsh we met in guest houses, overnight farmhouses (our favorite accommodations) and along the nation's clean highways with plenty of rest stops *were* pleasant.

The draw of Wales

We all know of celebrities from Wales: Dylan Thomas, Richard Burton, Laura Ashley, Tom Jones and the writer Jan Morris. Oh, and actor Anthony Hopkins, who spends most of the year in Los Angeles but is forever drawn back briefly to Wales.

Between making two of his recent films, "Nixon" and "Picasso," he relaxed in Wales, telling an interviewer, "Wales has a powerful and mixed landscape which could attract film companies — if only they knew where it was. With all due respect to the Americans, especially Hollywood Americans, I believe they think that Wales is in Ireland."

Even if they are advised it's on the southwest coast of Britain, they summon up "Wales as a place of piping tenors, thatched cottages, singing coal miners — the 1941 Hollywood version of 'How Green Was My Valley'."

If, occasionally, the Welsh were surprised we weren't exclaiming over their countryside — the hills, gentle rivers, valleys and stubby mountains — we had to remind them that back home in Vermont, our countryside wasn't that different. Okay, they had more grazing sheep — in fact, more sheep than people, whereas it's been 30 years since the cows exceeded humans where we live.

Mostly, we reveled in what we don't have at home: a seacoast, since Vermont is landlocked. And castles — oh, the splendid castles of Wales to which we sometimes returned to catch in that special light of late afternoon so kind to color film.

Marine Life Rescue Center

Perhaps it is appropriate that the highlight of our trip was not the superb Celtica Museum nor the Bodnant Garden, inland, but the seacoast with its notorious high tides.

The Tourist Office in Cardiff suggested that when we got down to Fishguard (from which ferries leave for Ireland) we might check out the Welsh Marine Life Rescue Center in nearby Milford Haven.

Every once in a while they rescue a stranded baby seal separated from its mother. More likely, they'd show us around and direct us to the bird and seal hospital where rescued seals are nursed back to health.

When we eventually reached Fishguard and put up for three days at the **Gilfach Goch Farmhouse** just east of town, we had June Devonwald (farmhouse proprietress, cook, cat lover, raconteur) phone ahead one morning. Yes, we could visit the Rescue Center; all was quiet, however.

But when we arrived at Terry and Anne Leadbetter's Rescue Center that morning, Terry was hitching up the rescue trailer to his 4x4. A call had come in about a stranded seal and Terry and his volunteer sidekick would soon be off to investigate. "Come along!"

In the back seat of the 4x4, we saw how locals navigate their roads — pedal to the metal, but always alert.

In no time we were bumping over sheep-grazing land, opening and closing wooden gates to pull up at the edge of a cliff with Atlantic surf pounding on rocky beach below reached by metal stairs.

It was there where Terry and his sidekick spotted a grayish baby seal in trouble — abandoned and malnourished. How Terry spotted

Two Welshmen out for a stroll near the shores of Cardigan Bay.

this seal, the same color as the rocks, is still a mystery.

Terry approached the seal from behind and managed to force open its jaws (seal bites can be nasty and sometimes poisonous).

Then they ran a clear plastic tube down the seal's throat. First, a pink liquid from a toothpaste-tube-sized container was forced into the hapless seal; two more containers followed.

The two did little talking, except to the seal, but we managed to learn the three infusions were nourishment, antibiotics and a mild tranquilizer, for the seal would be transported in a trailer cage to New Quay where Alan and Jean Bryant, alerted by cellular phone, would await our arrival at their Bird and Wildlife Hospital.

Nursing back to health

Like the Leadbetters, the Bryants are volunteers, running

their hospital by donations.

There, our rescued seal, still groggy, was weighed, named Glory and placed under a heat lamp.

We saw 14 other seals in various states of recovery. (Not all survive.) Some were lying in pens; others were near an indoor pool.

They must learn to swallow and catch fish and fatten up to at least 40 pounds before being returned to the sea.

No birds or other animals are kept for display at this sanctuary.

What made the day especially meaningful is that everyone involved was a volunteer. Terry and Anne make a modest living out of a dog-boarding kennel. The Bryants are referred to as "retired," but they are anything but.

The Royal Society for the Prevention of Cruelty to Animals (which Terry views critically) presented a citation to the Bryants four years ago for the care they'd given to seals, birds, badgers, otters and other wildlife at their hospital, which originally had been established to clean and rehabilitate oil-covered seabirds.

When we finally returned to our farmhouse, a bit late for our evening meal, we mused on how many baby seals are still today clubbed for their fur whereas we'd all spent the best part of a day rescuing a single, stranded seal.

You can bet we slept well in our farmhouse guest room that night.

Rental notes

The next day we had a leisurely drive to return to the car rental agency in Swansea. Our solid-black VW Golf (next time we'll request a lighter color to show up better on the country's black roads) was left off a bit dusty but lacking a scratch or a dent.

I'm sure Terry would jest that that was because of our 12-day "slow motion" driving tour. But we did manage to cover every section of Wales, from Cardiff up through Snowdonia to the Isle of Anglesey and down to St. David's.

Incidentally, there's an upper age limit of 75 for car rentals.

A passage in an 8-year-old Fodor's "Great Britain" lyrically makes the case for touring Wales in a car: "There is nothing to touch the freedom, enchantment and inspiration by motoring in the grass-banked, secret lanes of Wales — where the buses can't go — or near its wild and rocky coast. Apart from one's feet or a horse, it is the only way to see Wales."

Six-day sampler of Wales

KATHARINE McCORMACK, Tarzana, CA

In June of 1997, a woman friend and I took a bus (coach, to the British) tour of Wales. I made our plans using a British tour company, Frames-Rickards, in London. I dealt directly with them, feeling that that way it would be cheaper because no agent would be involved.

Getting started through England

I assumed that the other tour members would be, in the main, Britishers, but that proved not to be the case: of the 42 in the group there were four from South Africa, a few from Australia, a few from Canada and the rest Americans.

Patrons are on the honor system at this outdoor used-book stand in Hay-on-Wye.

The tour started on a Monday at 8 o'clock sharp, and Gladys and I made it by five minutes. It turned out that the driver was also the lecturer, and he managed the double duty very well indeed. The coach was a handsome, dark-red-and-gray vehicle with the usual amenities of a tour bus.

The only reservation I have concerning the comfort of the coach was that the lowest step was high off the ground and there were no handles or poles to assist one as he/she alighted or embarked the coach.

One woman, evidently having some inside knowledge, had brought a little box to stand on; otherwise, the driver was forced to assist the passengers who could not debark by themselves.

On the way to our first overnight stop, a hotel near Mold on the Welsh-British border, we passed through the little village of Bladon, where Churchill is buried, which is near Blenheim Palace where he was born.

Then it was on through the Vale of Evesham, with a distant glimpse of Worcester, to the fascinating old town of Ludlow. We stopped there for a pub lunch and a walk around the town, which has an outstanding castle.

Although Shrewsbury would have been interesting to wander around in, time would not allow, but we did get a good idea of its attractions. During this journey through England, John, the driver/guide, gave good commentary.

Castles and mountains

The hotel at Mold was unremarkable but served as our headquarters for a day spent sightseeing in northern Wales.

The first stop was Conwy, where there is a castle and very well-preserved walls.

Then we made our way over a spectacular pass to the coast and Caernarfon Castle, where the Prince of Wales was invested.

This was a 2-hour stop, which gave us time to walk around in the shell of this medieval castle and have a pub lunch at the *Castle Vaults* pub.

A good climb out of the town took us into Snowdonia National Park, where Mt. Snowdonia is famous for climbing and for the cog railway which ascends the mountain from Llanberis.

We, however, went on to Llangollen, which hosts an annual music festival called the Eisteddfod. On the way back to Mold we were treated to the magnificent scenery along the Horseshoe Pass; standing deep below are the ruins of Valle Crucis Abbey.

The third day found us in Porthmadog on the coast, and a narrow-gauge railway took us high into the mountains.

Just short of the terminus we reboarded the coach, which was waiting there to meet us, and headed for a now-defunct slate mine. This was a lunch stop, after which we had the opportunity to be carried through a portion of the mine on little cars, just for the sake of getting an idea of the hard life of slate miners in the 19th century.

The scenery around this mine was marred by piles of slate tailings that have piled up like little mountains. Bushes of rhododendrons pushing through the detritus seemed out of place.

The scenery improved dramatically as we entered the Elan Valley and were able to see the three reservoirs which provide water for the city of Birmingham in England. That night was spent in the comfortable, old Victorian hotel **Glen Usk** in Llandrindod Wells.

Heading south

From there we headed south, following the River Wye. The scenery was very different from that in the north, a gentle kind of beauty.

Our lunch destination was Hay-on-Wye, again on the border and a town famous for being the secondhand-book capital of the world — so called. We had about three hours to spend in this fascinating town.

Gladys and I separated, she to visit the cattle market and I to mosey around among the bookstores and sample a restaurant, *The Granary*, recommended by John, the driver.

Morris dancer at Tintern Abbey.

The seating in this rather large establishment was informal. I sat down at a long table and shortly was joined by a woman who said she always came in on market days. It was a perfect opportunity to get a feel for the way people live in this section.

This experience bolsters my theory that people traveling alone can many times derive more enjoyment from a situation than if they were with someone else.

Still following the River Wye, we passed through the town of Brecon. This was a lunch stop, and Gladys and I had ours in the yard of an old coaching inn. We then taxied to the cathedral, which was way too far away for a walk to it.

The coach then proceeded into Brecon Beacons National Park for one of the most scenic drives of the whole trip. Fortunately, the sun came out in full force as the coach crept along on a one-lane road.

That day, the fourth, finished with a visit to the Welsh Folk Museum at St. Fagans. The museum covers over 100 acres and traces the history of the country by means of a series of re-erected houses, farms and industrial buildings, all situated around an Elizabethan manor house.

A short journey through industrial South Wales ended in Cardiff, where we stayed at the **Forte Post House** right in Cardiff City.

Valle Cruces Abbey ruins as seen from Horsehoe Pass near Ruthin, Wales.

Cardiff and environs

Day five started out with a drive along a motorway to the west, ending up at the village of Laugharne, for many years home of the great Welsh poet and writer Dylan Thomas.

The coach parked near the ruins of a large castle and we made our way to Dylan's boathouse. We saw a video on the poet's life and then had a snack on a patio overlooking the estuary of the River Cymin.

The last stop on this day's tour was in the walled town of Tenby, a resort town with a lengthy esplanade overlooking the water.

We picked the *Five Arches Tavern* for our lunch and were happy we did, for set in the walls of the ladies' room was a bake oven, part of the original fortification. Certainly, experiences like that make history come alive.

Mostly sleeping our way back to Cardiff, we anticipated the medieval banquet at the castle. Before the banquet we were given a tour of some of the rooms in the new castle, built by a local tycoon in the last century.

Returning to London

On our way back to London the next day, the driver detoured north in a horseshoe route. Along the Wye, fields of rape lent color to river views. At the top of the horseshoe was the border town of Monmouth, where we glimpsed the Monnow Bridge on which stands a fortified gateway, unique in Britain.

Tintern Abbey was a lunch stop; moreover, we were fortunate enough to see a troop of Morris dancers going through their paces in colorful costumes. The head man told me the dancing was recreation for the dancers, who spent weekends going around to various villages.

Our tour company was Frames-Rickards, 11 Herbrand St., London WC1N 1EX England. From overseas, phone +44 171 837-3111. They will be glad to send a brochure describing this and other tours, including prices.

This tour cost the equal of $750 for six days, with first-class accommodations, breakfasts, dinners and all admissions.

Whimsical village of Portmeirion

RITA BERMAN, Chapel Hill, NC

As a writer, I find it of personal interest to seek out places that have literary or film connections. In the summer of 1995 when I visited family in England, I stayed mostly in the county of Sussex, about 90 miles south of London. However, I did venture to Wales to visit the whimsical "film set" village of Portmeirion.

The long route

I traveled from Sussex to Portmeirion by train, having bought a special England and Wales pass, standard class, for $155 before leaving the United States. This allowed four days of train travel within one month.

If London is your base, you can take a rapid Inter-City train from Euston station and reach Bangor, the nearest station to Portmeirion, in just under four hours.

However, because it was the weekend of May 8th, the V-E Day anniversary celebrations, I chose to avoid London and went cross-country, making my connections at Portsmouth, Bristol and Crewe. It took nine hours because of the waiting time between trains, but

View of the Gloriette and Piazza, with Telford's Tower on the right, Portmeirion.

it was an interesting journey.

The last leg of my journey was an hour-long taxi ride from Bangor through the mountains to the village of Portmeirion.

Italianate architecture

On a map of Wales, Portmeirion is south of Caernarfon on the west coast of Wales off A496.

Day and overnight visitors are drawn to this delightfully visual Italian-architecture village that was the site for the 1966-67 television series "The Prisoner," which starred Patrick McGoohan and Leo McKern. Cottage Number Six, which was used as the exterior of the prisoner's home, is now a shop specializing in items relating to the series.

The village is open all year. The entrance fees for day visitors are £3 (near US$4.80) for adults and £1.50 ($2.40) for children five years and older.

After the day visitors have gone, the village becomes quiet and can be safely enjoyed in an unhurried way. I took long walks on the trails and the wide sands of the estuary. There was a profusion of flowers and in the background I could see the mountains across the estuary.

Built on a secluded peninsula in Cardigan Bay, the village grew from an idea of architect Sir Clough Williams-Ellis that "one could develop even a very beautiful place without defiling it." The village is a wonderful conglomeration of cottages, towers, arches, statues, piazzas and clever visual illusions, interwoven with trees, plants and shrubs.

Bits and pieces of old buildings, abandoned objects, follies and whimsical items were used in the making of the village, which took from 1925 to 1927 to complete. Unlike modern-day development, trees were spared, as the cottages were designed to blend in with the natural environment.

Writers have been drawn to Portmeirion. Noël Coward wrote "Blithe Spirit" there in 1941 and H.G. Wells, George Bernard Shaw and Bertrand Russell were earlier visitors.

Lodging choice

I spent three days at **Hotel Portmeirion**, a comfortable Victorian-type villa. The hotel offered a special 2-night break, so my superior single room cost £125 ($194) per night inclusive of dinner and breakfast.

Someone wrote in the hotel guest book that the chef, Craig Hindley, was "an artist, not a cook." Not only was the food delicious but it was beautifully arranged on the plate. Dining is unhurried, as dishes are cooked individually to order.

I enjoyed such main courses as a roast Trelough duck, loin of Welsh lamb with provencale vegetables and a basil-and-olive sauce, and a red snapper braised in a vegetable-and-aniseed bouillon.

Ffestiniog Railway

A short taxi ride and I was outside of Portmeirion in nearby Porthmadog. This modern town sits in the shadow of the Snowdon range of mountains. Porthmadog has a harbor, marine museum, lots of little shops and two narrow-gauge railways.

The Ffestiniog Railway runs 13½ miles into the mountains to Blaenau Ffestiniog. On the road to the next town of Tremadog is the Christian Mountain Centre; this house was the birthplace of T.E. Lawrence (Lawrence of Arabia).

I took the Ffestiniog steam train up into the Snowdonia mountains. This railway is a tourist attraction

The village of Portmeirion, Wales.

run mostly by volunteers. An interesting feature of the line is the rail spiral at Dduallt, the only one in Great Britain where the railway crosses over itself to gain height.

The train goes through tunnels and passes the hydroelectric power station. Along the route there are stops to allow passengers access to nature trails and walks.

The weather had turned cold that day, so when we reached the end of the line at Blaenau Ffestiniog I decided it was too blustery to visit the Llechwedd slate mines and Victorian village.

Instead, I stayed on the train and returned to Porthmadog. By paying extra for first class, £16.60 ($26) round trip, I had a large, comfortable armchair from which to enjoy the view.

For reservations and room rates, contact Hotel Portmeirion, Portmeirion, Gwynedd, LL48 6ET, Wales; phone 01766 770228.

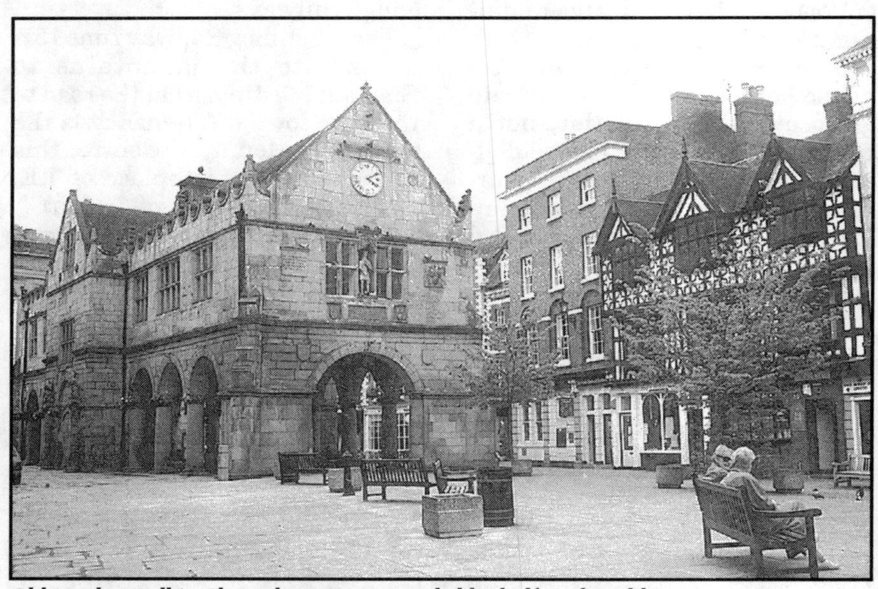

Old Market Hall in Shrewsbury is surrounded by half-timbered houses.

When in Wales, do as the Welsh do

GLADYS L. SHARP, Running Springs, CA

It wasn't the castles in Wales that drew us to Britain in May, although there are castles aplenty, some mere ruins, others beautifully restored and quite livable.

It surely wasn't the weather, because in 1996 Britain experienced the coldest and wettest May in 350 years. Of course, we couldn't have known how rainy it would be; usually May is lovely there.

What did draw us to Wales was the opportunity to vacation as the Welsh do, to enjoy their recreational areas with our Welsh friends.

Canal boating

We had heard of boating on the numerous canals that wind through the British countryside, and the four of us thought that might be a great adventure.

Building canals became a craze about 200 years ago and, in Britain, builders vied to create new transportation routes to carry the tremendous cargo generated by the Industrial Revolution. Over 2,000 miles of these waterways are still navigable and, with their locks, tunnels, lift bridges and aqueducts, they appear much the same as they did two centuries ago.

Today the canals are popular as an escape from the stresses of daily life. They are no longer profitable for carrying cargo because of their limited capacity (many locks are only seven feet wide by 70 feet long). Thousands of people spend their leisure hours on narrowboats that ply these old canals.

Most of Britain's major cities are linked by these waterways that wend through tiny villages, busy market towns and peaceful, gentle countryside. It is estimated that there are about 20,000 pleasure boats plying these canals, most of them built in the traditional narrowboat style.

There's more to the canals than just a network for navigation. Because they were built before the internal combustion engine, the early boats were towed by horses along the adjacent towpath. Today, hikers along these paths make their way through glens and valleys of wondrous beauty. Quaint towns and vintage pubs line the canals, offering opportunities to step back in time and enjoy life as lived by the British in the 19th century.

Late in 1995 we contacted Le Boat, Inc., at 10 S. Franklin Turnpike, Ste. 204B, Ramsey, NJ 07446; phone 800/992-0291, the U.S. agents for Black Prince Narrowboat Holidays of England. They provided brochures and planning for the great adventure began.

Many choices

There are over 80 companies renting boats that ply the network of canals in middle and western England and eastern Wales, with a variety of narrowboats, many different routes available and several marinas from which to depart. On every canal the boaters must raise and lower locks and bridges.

Some routes are decidedly more difficult than others and we chose the easiest possible. *Easy* was important to us because the four of us are all over 60 and our friend has had two heart by-pass surgeries.

The Llangollen Canal runs from Wales into western England and was our choice because it has but one lift bridge and just four locks, two up and two back. Perfect for us.

This canal, a section of the Shropshire Union Canal, has been called one of the most spectacular stretches of inland waterway in Britain — especially where it crosses the Dee Valley on the Pontcysyllte Aqueduct.

Because you carry all your home comforts with you, a boating holiday is a civilized adventure. An adventure it is, because around every corner there is something new to see or do as the canal winds alongside lovely old towns and villages, stately homes, interesting museums and bustling cities.

Children and adults alike enjoy this relaxed, yet busy, holiday.

The Black Prince company makes boating with them easy. They even make available a list of foodstuffs from which you may order, if you wish. These foods will be on the boat when you take possession. They now have available one-way and 3-day trips in addition to the regular one- and 2-week routes.

Boats were available to new occupants Saturdays after 4 o'clock, so after a pleasant drive from Cardiff to Shropshire, past Oswestry, we arrived at the Chirk Marina well before time.

Our narrowboat, the *AYR*, intimidated us at first. Because it was six feet wide and 60 feet long, the fellows felt it might be difficult to maneuver. Their previous boating experience consisted only of manning a 2-man fishing boat and owning a 24-foot cabin cruiser.

The marina personnel provided a modicum of instruction; a girl of 18 took us on a tour of the boat, pointing out the stove, TV, engine and other important features of our home-to-be for a week.

A male employee started the engine, took the boat out of the marina into the canal and started us on our way. He jumped off the boat at the first bridge and made his way along the footpath back to the marina to indoctrinate others just beginning their week's adventure.

The adventure begins

All too soon we were on our own, but we loved it. Chugging along at the breakneck speed of four miles an hour, there was time to look and to ooh and aah at the green, green meadows and undulating hills.

Not long after leaving the marina we encountered the lift bridge. Our friend steered the boat near the bank so my husband could jump off and raise the bridge, then the rest of us floated under the bridge. After returning the bridge to the correct position, he jumped back on and we continued merrily on our way.

We bumped and scraped our way along the narrow canal and went over the 1,000-foot-long Pontcysyllte Aqueduct, an 18th-century engineering masterpiece by Thomas Telford which rises 126 feet above the Dee Valley.

After maneuvering a wide turn, we finally reached Llangollen where the canal was lined with boats moored for the night. Boats must be moored by dusk; we were fortunate to secure the last available spot in town.

Here the mooring places had water and toilets available; other stopping places are not so well equipped. (We did not need these facilities, but others do.)

Llangollen mooring

Llangollen, a charming old town with many half-timbered houses and inviting walkways, lies mostly below the canal and is its western terminus. On our first foray we walked along the canal to lovely Horseshoe Falls, cruised the town for postcards, then returned to the warm boat, glad to be in out of the drizzle and cold.

There is an excellent, award-winning Canal Exhibition Centre at Llangollen. The town is also famous for the International *Eisteddfod,* a colorful festival of

The AYR, our narrowboat home, moored in Ellsmere along the Llangollen Canal.

music and dance that attracts participants from over 30 nations.

On a stretch of canal from which narrowboats are restricted, children and those young in heart can ride a horse-drawn open canal boat like those used to carry cargo in the 18th century — a great glimpse into days gone by.

The next day, Sunday, it rained all day and we opted to stay put, not wishing to have one or both helmsmen outside in the cold and wet. (We hope on our next trip the weather encourages more walking and sightseeing.)

Our diesel-powered *AYR* was comfortable and dry and completely self-contained. The narrow galley was a one-person kitchen, but the living room was ample and the two bedrooms with joining bath as comfortable as one could expect in a 6-foot-wide boat. The bunks in the rear bedroom were quite narrow and our friend, who is not small, said he had to get out of bed to roll over.

By Sunday evening the rain lessened, so we walked into town proper and ate in a nice pub. Even though the day had been gray and gloomy, the beauty of the Vale of Llangollen awed us.

Along the canal

Monday was cold, but the sun shone most of the time. We were ready to retrace our way back over the aqueducts, and past the marina from which we had started, to see what lay in the other direction.

A fierce, cold wind blew and foiled many turns as it slammed against the broadside of the narrowboat. Just when the fellows had the boat going correctly, a heavy gust would slam against the barge and push it the wrong direction.

After a bit of stress and frustration we made it onto and over the Pontcysyllte and Chirk aqueducts, past the marina, through a 400-meter-long tunnel, and then in and out of two sets of locks.

We moored for the night at a wide spot in the canal only a few yards from an attractive pub, *The Poacher's Pocket*.

Beautiful ducks escorted us along the canal; we were especially enamored with the flamboyant mandarin ducks and their drab hens mothering their numerous downy offspring.

Along the canal, wildflowers in tangled profusion clung to the banks, flowers I'd never heard of like coocoo pints and cow parsley, which looks something like Queen Anne's Lace.

Nettles, tall sturdy grasses and gorse lined the banks, which were always green. In some places graceful willows bent over the canal, dipping fingertips into the water — just for fun. Primroses, hanging in Babylon gardens, intermingling with tiny violets decorated the waterway. In spots it was almost jungle-like, with one green attempting to overpower another.

We think this country beautiful beyond telling, even during unpleasant weather.

Ellesmere was a lovely stopping place, though the rain slowed our discovery of its delights. Here we opted to stay two nights.

If for nothing else, we remember Ellesmere for the wonderful anniversary dinner we enjoyed at *The Cellar*, a first-class restaurant — quite unexpected in such a small town. Don't be put off by the entrance; inside, the ambiance and food are worthy of London's best.

The duckling and the grilled salmon were delicious and the vegetables cooked to perfection.

Hikers along these former tow paths make their way through glens and valleys of wondrous beauty.

We began the dinner with deep-fried camembert and ended with crème caramel and a fruit torte. For the four of us this wonderful dinner came to £40, or about $60, including beverages.

Picturesque Shrewsbury

The next day we hired a car and driver and spent a delightful day in Shrewsbury, home of Brother Cadfael and his adventures. Although the Cadfael film series was filmed in Hungary (for financial reasons), the abbey and the town take full advantage of the publicity and revere their famous author, Ellis Peters. The abbey is unpretentious but welcoming, especially in the rain.

In Old Town there are many 15th- and 16th-century, black-and-white half-timbered buildings, some of which, like the Rowley House, have been turned into interesting museums. Shrewsbury is well worth a return visit.

It was Thursday when we headed back toward the marina, again stopping for the night alongside the *Poacher's Pocket*, where we enjoyed a savory dinner in a family pub with atmosphere. Dinners ranged from £4.75 to £7.55 (or about $7.50 to $12). The address is Glendrid, Chirk, Oswestry LL14 5DQ; phone 01691 773250.

With honest regrets we bade good-bye to our floating home, the *AYR*. If only we'd had regular May weather, the adventure would have been absolutely perfect instead of merely wonderful.

Facts and figures

For our well-appointed Duchess Class Narrowboat from Black Prince, the prices ranged from $965 in low season to $1,640 in high season. Other smaller boats ranged from $710 to $1,215 and larger narrowboats with berths for 10 persons ranged from $1,030 to $2,045.

British Waterways has an official website at *www.britishwaterways.org*.

Renting a cottage on the Welsh coast

GLADYS L. SHARP, Running Springs, CA

In a lovely cottage on the Pembrokeshire Coast we spent the last week of our Welsh vacation. Our friends had made all arrangements for rental of a charming refurbished milking house sited on a working farm. The building was beautifully restored and remodeled into a deluxe 3-bedroom home with all the amenities — dishwasher, laundry, even color TV.

This cottage, **Sea Maidens**, was only a half mile from Abereiddi Beach. From here we made day trips to surrounding towns and sights. Rental prices for these attractive cottages ranged from £250 to £350 ($400-$560) per week.

Contact Wales Cottage Holidays; their telephone number in Wales is 01686 628200.

Historic sights

Of special interest to all of us were the Cathedral of St. David

Sea Maidens, a remodled milking house in Pembrokeshire, now serves as a lovely cottage.

and the ruins of the Bishop's Palace in the small seacoast city of St. Davids. The church has a very old foundation; there has probably been a church on that site since the sixth century. The present building has been in continuous usage since the 12th century.

Photo opportunities abound; the grounds of the venerable buildings are beautiful. Inside, we were awed by the incredible carved-wood ceilings, a magnificent old organ and numerous lovely chapels.

Another day, we visited an Iron Age fort and Pentre Ifan, a prehistoric burial chamber. We were fortunate the rain was a mere drizzle and didn't impede our search into history.

Closer to our holiday cottage we toured a local cheese factory, Llangloffan Farmhouse Cheese Centre, where the owner/guide provided insights into both cheese making and politics — an interesting two hours.

Other attractions

The Welsh National Footpath ran through the farm where we stayed and one day we squished and slogged our way through a meadow, complete with cows and bulls, then climbed a stile to reach the little village of Abereiddi Beach. Only a few stone cottages and a street of ruined row houses built for miners' families mark the once-busy slate-mining village.

The spectacular Blue Lagoon, a deep inlet of the ocean that figured importantly in the slate-mining process, draws many visitors to the otherwise forgettable village whose beach is not sand but tide-polished stones that make scrambling along the beach an unpleasant experience. Other nearby beaches are sandy and encourage sunbathing and playing.

A mile from Sea Maidens we located a lovely pub, *Artamont Arms*, where the delicious food was charmingly served in the dining room by a lad of about 17. A second visit only confirmed our opinion: this is a pub worth patronizing. Dinners with beverage and dessert cost under £10 ($16).

Rhododendrons

All too soon our week was over and we headed back to Penarth to rest up for our trip home. There was one more park they wanted to show us, one where rhododendrons grows trees (not bushes) so prolific and hardy that a corps of gardeners works constantly to keep them under control.

The size of the blooms (six inches in diameter), the myriad colors and the profusion of blossoms on each tree astounded us. Just another jewel in the beauty of Wales, and a reminder of the rain necessary to keep it so lovely.

Brighton and Chartwell

Reluctantly, we bade our Welsh friends good-bye and moved on to England via a bus that runs directly from Cardiff to Heathrow and Gatwick. Traveling by bus is fast and convenient; however, be sure to buy a round-trip ticket for only one pound more than the one-way fare.

Friends, who live only a half hour from Gatwick Airport took us in hand for a couple days, introducing us to this lovely corner of England.

The Royal Pavilion at Brighton, with its fanciful minarets and highly ornamented interior, amused us. We spent several enjoyable hours there before driving through the countryside aflame with yellow rape, the seeds of which are used for the cooking oil we call canola oil. These blossoms

Amid lovely surroundings, St. Davids Cathedral and the ruins of the Bishop's Palace are worth a visit.

must be the yellowest yellow we've ever seen — a spectacular sight from air or road.

The following day we toured Chartwell, the home of Winston Churchill. Here we felt like we were visiting the home of friends; it was comfortable and homey, not at all like the Pavilion with its ornate decor.

We enjoyed dinner at another noteworthy pub, the *Rose and Crown*, in Fletching. Here, the dining room was rustic but elegant, the service personal and cheerful and the food outstanding and beautifully presented. Dinners, with beverage and dessert, ran between £10 and £12 ($16-$19).

Four weeks after landing in England, we reluctantly departed. It had been, for us, a very different vacation, but most enjoyable, experiencing a variety of pleasures with our Welsh friends.

Dylan Thomas country — a Welsh inspiration

RITA BERMAN©, Chapel Hill, NC

In April 1998 I exchanged my time-share week in North Carolina for a week in Laugharne, Wales, staying at **The Seasons** at Laugharne Park, a 40-acre time-share resort overlooking the sweep of Carmarthen Bay, in order to visit the Boat House, former home of writer and poet Dylan Thomas.

Inspirational setting

A friend and I traveled by car from the south coast of England, but for those who are coming directly from Heathrow airport, Laugharne is about 217 miles. By car, take the M4 west to Carmarthen and then the A40 to St. Clears; turn off onto the A4066 to Laugharne. If you are planning on visiting Cardiff, Laugharne is only 80 miles west of Cardiff.

The marsh, the salty sea and sense of place all featured in Thomas's work. Like many a writer he mined his environment for inspiration, and at Laugharne there is plenty to inspire.

From the windows of our lodge, we had a clear view of the estuary. Every day we enjoyed the changing scenery that occurred when the tide came in or went out, and on a clear day we could see not only the surrounding areas but across to England's North Devon coast.

The lodge was nicely furnished and had a fully equipped kitchen, so we prepared most of our meals and ate dinner out only once. We soon discovered that the coin meter needed constant feeding if we were to have hot water and heat.

From the living room we could see another lodge below us, off to the right slightly. A pair of chimney swifts appeared to be building a nest in the chimney and provided a source of entertainment for us during the week as we observed their behavior whenever other birds came near. Seagulls often hovered in the vicinity.

Going out of Laugharne, on the "down" street — view from St. Martin's Church.

Spring seemed to be later in arriving at Wales than in the south of England, and the trees outside our windows were bare when we first arrived but had begun to leaf out by the time we left a week later.

On Sunday we drove to nearby St. Clears to shop for food, but we had trouble locating any stores that were open. In our search for food we also drove to Pembroke, a castle town, and Tenby, which is an ancient walled town.

Dylan's haunts

Laugharne is composed of two parts, an "up street" and a "down street." Up street is the area between the church and Laugharne Castle, where most of the best buildings are to be found, while down street has small cottages and a few merchant homes dating back to the days when it was a busy little port.

Walking around Laugharne, you can see where roads have been built over the Coran stream that runs into the River Taf; signs warn visitors that certain areas such as The Strand parking lot near the castle get flooded with high tide.

The footpath from The Strand that leads to the Boat House on the riverbank, where Dylan and his wife, Caitlin, lived from 1949 to 1953, is accessible only at certain times of the day. A longer route from the town center takes you along Market Lane to Dylan's Walk and provides superb views of the estuary.

From that location I could understand what Thomas meant

when he described the 3-story house as a "sea shaken house on a breakneck of rocks." It perches precariously on the cliff edge, high over the sea, with nothing to interrupt the view.

I looked into the writing shed where he had worked. It was originally a garage and has windows overlooking the estuary. His poem "Over Sir John's Hill" utilizes the view from these windows.

Another day we hiked on a footpath that went through the woods and then took us upriver, skirting a farmyard. At some point we lost the path, or else it had been obliterated because of the horses churning up the land. Crossing some fields, we found ourselves near St. Martin's Church where Dylan Thomas is buried in a simple grave with a plain white cross.

From this street I photographed the small cottages that lead into the grander Clifton and King streets where the buildings are mainly Georgian.

Brown's Hotel, one of Dylan's favorite haunts, is located on King Street. Opposite it are some cottages, one being "The Pelican" where Dylan Thomas's parents lived. Another cottage has been turned into a bookstore.

Walking around Laugharne, we passed by the dramatic-looking Laugharne Castle, which was opened to the public in 1995 after extensive restoration and excavation. It was one of a string of fortresses guarding the ancient route along the south Wales coast

For a time, Dylan and Caitlin stayed at the Hughes' house alongside Laugharne Castle.

"I have the romantic, dirty summerhouse looking over the marsh to write in, and Caitlin an almost empty, huge room to dance in," he wrote to his friend Vernon Watkins.

This was where he compiled "Portrait of the Artist as a Young Dog." We also saw the now rundown looking "Sea View" house which had been an earlier home for Thomas and Caitlin.

Not-on-the-map Cenarth

Another day we drove to Cenarth, a small village off the A484. On the way we passed through Carmarthen and Newcastle Emlyn. Old Cenarth is an ancient village which was in existence in 1188 when Gerald Cambrensis passed through when he recruited men for the second crusade.

For centuries Cenarth was the center of coracle fishing. Coracles are small boats made from wicker frames, usually covered with hide or leather. They are small enough for an individual to carry on his back.

A collection of coracles from all over the world may be seen at the National Coracle Center, which is on the grounds of a 17th-century flour mill adjacent to the Salmon Leap Waterfalls. A 200-year-old bridge spans the river Teifi. The village is now designated a conservation area.

There is an interesting Old Smithy Craftshop and Heritage Centre. The attached stone cottage was originally a vicarage and later housed the village school. At Cenarth we found a nice little tea shop and had tea and Welsh cakes, which are cooked on a griddle and served with butter or jam.

From Cenarth we proceeded to the market town of Cardigan and

The Boat House as seen from the cliff path.

looked at the bay, then on to Fishguard, a harbor town from where the ferries to Ireland depart.

Coastal walk

For a change of pace, we decided to take a walk in the coastal area.

Starting off early one morning, we took the "Lacques" public footpath from Laugharne and walked by the side of the river stream, through muddy areas and across a field until we came out on the road to Pendine. We ate lunch in a field, then continued our walking along the main road.

Most of the coastal area between the road and the sea had been taken over by the Ministry of Defence, and barbed wire and fences prevented our getting through to the sea.

Closer to Pendine, we saw many caravans for sale and on site. Pendine boasts a Museum of Speed, a few shops and the **Beach Hotel**. I couldn't figure out why anyone would want to stay there, except that the flatness of the beach provided a safe place to bathe and accommodation might be cheap because of the number of caravans.

From Pendine we caught a bus back to Laugharne.

Lofty hiking

The next morning, Thursday, was to be our most strenuous walking day. Returning to Pendine by car, we located a parking spot and then started the upward climb on the Pembrokeshire Coast footpath.

It was a lovely, sunny day and we had a bird's-eye view of the land as we walked high above the sea on the cliffs. Down below us was a little bay, called Pelle Bay.

Unfortunately, we appeared to have strayed from the official path so made our descent across fields of gorse and flattened grass to the bay, where we rested and took a lunch break. On making our trek upward we found the path again and continued on it toward Amroth and then back to Pendine.

From the clifftop we saw the broad swath of the Pendine Sands, which was the site of land-speed record attempts by Sir Malcolm Campbell and Parry Thomas in the 1920s. The Museum of Speed includes exhibits of Thomas's restored car "Babs" and other vehicles.

My friend had brought along shooting sticks, which are walking sticks each with a spike to pierce the ground and a thin strip of canvas at the top that opens out to make a small seat. These were very helpful, not only in establishing a safe footing on the cliff path but also as a means of taking the weight off our backs and legs when we paused.

At times, I found the clifftop height a bit scary, especially as no handrails or fence separated us from a sheer drop down.

Boat House museum

Friday morning, we explored the western area by car, visiting Pembroke Docks, Milford Haven and up toward St. Davids, returning via Fishguard where we ate lunch in a little tea shop.

In the afternoon we toured the Boat House museum, paying the senior-citizen entrance fee of £1.5 ($2.50) each. It's open daily, and in the summer the last admission is at 5 p.m. An audiovisual presentation provides a good introduction for those unfamiliar with Thomas's history.

There are some original furnishings and memorabilia, including letters from President Jimmy Carter and others.

From inside the house I got yet another perspective of the estuary. Reading the comments from the visitors' book, I saw that others had found the house to be "peaceful, inspiring, a pilgrimage." One person wrote, "gone forever," and another, "magical, instructive." It was all of these things and more to me.

Laugharne accommodations

Accommodation note: The Seasons Resort is available to timeshare members only. Exchanges may be made through RCI; 800/338-7777.

Other accommodations in Laugharne may be found at, to name a few. . .

- **The Swan Cottage** bed-and-breakfast; phone 011-441-994-427409.
- **Strand Cottage**, a self-catering fisherman's cottage; phone 011-441-239-881244.
- **Sir John's Hill Farm** holiday cottages; phone 011-441-994-427667.

The Tourist Information Center, Carmarthen, publishes a guide to the area and offers a bed booking service; phone 011-441-267-231557.

Index